CHRISTIAN MUTUAL AID

A Handbook of Brotherhood Economics

SECTION FOR MENNONITE AID
PUBLICATION NUMBER 3

By

J. WINFIELD FRETZ

WIPF & STOCK · Eugene, Oregon

Wipf and Stock Publishers
199 W 8th Ave, Suite 3
Eugene, OR 97401

Christian Mutual Aid
A Handbook of Brotherhood Economics
By Fretz, Joseph Winfield and Bender, Harold S.
Softcover ISBN-13: 978-1-7252-8369-5
Hardcover ISBN-13: 978-1-7252-8367-1
eBook ISBN-13: 978-1-7252-8371-8
Publication date 6/25/2020
Previously published by Mennonite Central Committee, 1947

This edition is a scanned facsimile of the original edition published in 1947.

Table of Contents

	PAGE
Foreword	3

CHAPTER I
Introductory Comments About Mutual Aid 5

CHAPTER II
Mutual Aid is a Fundamental Principle of Nature 10

CHAPTER III
The Bible and Mutual Aid 16

CHAPTER IV
Our Forefathers Believed in Mutual Aid 23

CHAPTER V
Our Forefathers Practiced Mutual Aid 31

CHAPTER VI
Mennonites Practice Mutual Aid Today 38

CHAPTER VII
Mennonites Practice Mutual Aid Today—Continued 50

CHAPTER VIII
Present Day Needs for Mutual Aid 62

CHAPTER IX
Organizing Mutual Aid in the Local Community 72

CHAPTER X
What Mutual Aid Can Mean to the Church 82

Foreword

This booklet has been written to foster the development of a program of mutual aid among Mennonites. It assumes that the Mennonites in their various groups constitute Christian brotherhoods based upon a personal experience of faith in Jesus Christ as Saviour and Lord and a loving fellowship in His body, the Church. On this foundation it advocates that the members of the Christian community, locally and as a whole, bear one another's economic burdens and so not only fulfill the law of Christ but strengthen the Brotherhood for its greater tasks of witnessing and building for Christ in the world of today. It is a conscious effort to challenge the secular trend of the times which threatens to denature the Christian community and make its members increasingly dependent upon the state and the commercial world with consequent transfer of loyalty from the church to other agencies.

In this undertaking, the author is squarely within the authentic historic tradition of the Anabaptist-Mennonite movement with its spirit of Christian stewardship, mutual burden-bearing, and practical brotherly aid. Mennonites have always held that this spirit is the direct and necessary consequence of true Christian love, although they have not always practiced this ideal. The author is also entirely within the New Testament ideal, for what he advocates is a historic Christian principle anchored both in tradition and Scripture, and successfully applied at many times and places, both within and without the Mennonite brotherhood, though also often forgotten, neglected or deliberately by-passed for selfish profit.

There are increasing signs of a revival among the Mennonites in the practical application of brotherly mutual aid in various areas of common life and need. These applications range all the way from overseas colonization on a large scale to the granting of small loans to ex-CPS men, and the growth of local groups for mutual aid in such emergencies as illness, death and burial. In this revival, the author of this booklet has played no small part by his own contributions in vision, research and practical leadership, both in his own conference and in the larger circles of the total Mennonite constituency. He is now serving as chairman of the Mennonite Aid Section of the Mennonite Central Committee.

The demand for a convenient and practical summary of mutual aid principles, together with practical suggestions for procedure, has led the Mennonite Central Committee to prepare this booklet for wide circulation among our people and among others who might be interested in the application of Christian love and brotherhood to the economic aspect of our common life. The author has successfully combined Scripture teaching with historical illustrations and practical operating suggestions to produce a clear, concise, and helpful manual. We commend it to our ministerial and lay leadership in the hope that it will meet a real need and will give effective impetus to the growing revival of the practice of Christian mutual aid.

                THE MENNONITE CENTRAL COMMITTEE

                Harold S. Bender

June, 1947.

I

Introductory Comments About Mutual Aid

"God created man in his own image, in the image of God created he him." Genesis 1:27.

Mutual aid is a very old practice in human history. We may say that aid is mutual when two or more individuals work together to achieve a common good. Mutual Aid is a reciprocal process in that it benefits all parties concerned, in other words, the beneficial currents flow simultaneously in opposite directions. The idea of working together to accomplish desired goals is much older than the idea of working alone. In a very real sense mutual aid is a fundamental law of the universe. As such it is an inherent part of God's creation.

The earliest historical records reveal that ancient peoples lived in groups such as small communities, tribes, and families. They had a very simple way of life in comparison with the complex and highly intricate life of today. Yet an essential characteristic of their way of life was their sharing of the dangers, the sorrows, the joys and the bounties of life with one another. The extreme individualism so characteristic of modern life was utterly unknown to ancient peoples. It is not found today among the more simple cultures and civilizations.

Mutual Aid and Cooperation

In many ways the terms *mutual aid* and *cooperation* are synonymous. They may be used interchangeably. Some people would define mutual aid as "the idea of innate cooperation." While mutual aid is always cooperation, cooperation may sometimes not be mutual aid. The distinction, though subtle, must be made. It often happens that two or more individuals cooperate with one another to attain a common goal but they do so for basically selfish purposes. This is illustrated in our highly interdependent economic system of today where employer and employee, consumers and producers, professional men and their clients, may cooperate to attain a particular objective, but strictly speaking, one could not define it as mutual aid because the motives may be basically selfish. The primary concern of each group is for the welfare of itself and not for the other. In genuine Christian mutual aid, there is as much concern for the other person or group as for one's own. Wherever mutual aid is practiced, it is concerned with the total good rather than with the partial good. In other words, the group welfare will take precedence over the individual welfare.

Mutual Aid and Cooperatives

In America as well as in other countries there are cooperative organizations as well as mutual aid societies. Mutual aid societies may be characterized by the intimate nature of the relationships of the members and generally have as their primary motivation a religious or fraternal basis. Cooperative organizations are all too generally economically motivated and entirely secular in character. Basically, of course, the name of an organization or an activity is not important. The name does not make it good or bad, desirable or undesirable. Both cooperatives and mutual aid organizations may be selfishly or unselfishly motivated. The important thing to discover in trying to understand any organization is its primary purpose and its basic motives. Why do people belong? What do members expect to get out of the organization? What do they expect to contribute to it?

Our concern in the discussion of the topic of mutual aid is that we as Christian people who talk about being good neighbors, and about brotherhood and stewardship, and about serving Christ, actually make a transfer from religious ideals and doctrinal professions to our everyday work and business practices. It is our concern that our businesses are operated and our jobs filled with the same pure spirit and the same high purposes with which we operate our churches. Our prayer is that all these things be done in the name of Christ for the glory of God. As church workers, we serve not for personal profit and prestige, but because there is need of our time and our energy and our service for God's work. As Christians we must strive for the things we pray for. "Thy kingdom come. Thy will be done on earth as it is in heaven." We are co-workers together with God. A living faith is a working faith.

Mutual aid, like competition, is a form of striving but in the case of mutual aid it is striving with others to achieve a common good rather than striving against others for the sake of gaining personal advantage. Of course, not all forms of competition are necessarily harmful. The motives behind the striving in every case determine whether they are good or bad, harmful or helpful.

Mutual Aid is Not Charity

It is important that a distinction be made between mutual aid and charity. We have said that mutual aid is a two-way relationship in which currents of service flow in two directions. Charity is often a one-way relationship where the currents of service flow only in one direction. The rich give to the poor; the well-fed give to the hungry; those clothed in silk give to those in rags. The two groups are likely to have little in common. They tend to live each in a world apart. Those who have are likely to look pityingly and all too often with condescension upon those who have not. Those who are in need are likely to look with mixed feelings of gratitude and covetousness upon those from whom they receive. There is little the two groups have in common.

The people who constantly receive have no way of repaying those who give. Therefore, they tend to lose self-respect and often, respect for those from whom they receive as well. Let us put ourselves in the shoes of those who receive charity and see whether we could retain our own self-respect if over a period of time we would be recipients only. Most worthy people do not like to be on the receiving end of charity very long. They generally accept charity in the hope that it will reestablish them and make them able to be self-sufficient.

As givers, we frequently never really see the people to whom we give. We are not in face to face relationship with them. The giving is, therefore, impersonal. We give to a cause rather than to an individual and we continue giving never knowing whether we pauperize the individual or whether we rehabilitate him.

The loss of self-respect through constant receiving of charity was illustrated in the depression years by people who preferred to starve slowly rather than accept relief. To accept relief would have meant a loss of self-respect and a loss of group-respect.

In this pamphlet we are concerned with mutual aid rather than charity. Each has its place in the program of the church, but mutual aid, unlike charity, has been very much a stranger in the program of the current church. The purpose of mutual aid is to help needy church people to help themselves rather than to give them direct relief. Mutual Aid is a program designed to help set people on their own feet economically and spiritually so that they can in turn become stronger members of the Christian body and bear their share of the load in church and community. As Paul says: "But that as a matter of equality your abundance at the present time should supply their want, so that their abundance may supply your want, that there may be equality." II Cor. 8:14.

Why the Church is Interested in Mutual Aid

The primary function of the church is to preach the gospel of salvation to all mankind. The church is the organized body of believers in Jesus Christ and as such it must preach repentance from sin, but it must also teach its own members right ways of living and earning a living. It must be concerned with showing the "better way" of which Paul speaks.

A basic assumption underlying this pamphlet and the accompanying emphasis on mutual aid among Mennonites is that the Mennonite Church desires to continue teaching and practicing the doctrines of separation of church and state; of non-resistance, of non-conformity to a secular world and of simplicity of living. This assumption must be accepted in order to appreciate the purpose of this pamphlet which is to encourage the development of a program of Christian mutual aid among Mennonites. This emphasis is a conscious effort to move in an opposite direction to the secular currents of our time. It assumes that the church as a brotherhood can and will meet as many of its problems independent of government assistance as possible; that the church will accept increasingly less rather than more by way of patronage, favors, and financial advantage from the state; and that it will seek to meet its economic and social needs through mutual assistance on the part of its people. In other words, it assumes that the Mennonite Church wants to urge its members not to look to the government to supply all human needs from the cradle to the grave. Nor does it desire to give its members occasion to transfer their loyalties from the Christian Church to the secular state because the state promises to assume responsibility for all their economic needs.

To prevent this transfer of loyalty, it is important that a program of mutual aid be developed. A program in which the methods employed are based on the ethics of the New Testament rather than the standards derived from Hollywood, Fifth Avenue or Wall Street. A program characterized in Exodus 16:18, "He that gathered much had nothing over and he that gathered little had no lack." A program where brothers in Christ may indeed be free to act as brothers; where the daily functions of life are carried out not according to the secular commercial laws of the market, but rather according to the divine law of love.

As Christians, we hardly realize how far we have discarded the laws of Christ in favor of the laws of the market. In fact, many make no distinction between the two. The aim of this pamphlet is to help Christian people discover ways of aiding one another in Christ. Christian mutual aid is a program aimed to spiritualize our economic practices; to put a soul into our vocation and daily work.

In conclusion then we can define mutual aid as Christian love in action, as an aspect of the Christian way of life. It is using the resources God has given us for His glory and the good of ourselves and our fellow men. It is a way of limiting selfish desires for the good of the larger group or the community of which we are members. The spirit of mutual aid is well expressed in the following verse:

Would That Men Were Brotherly As Trees

In every patch of timber you
Will always find a tree or two
That would have fallen long ago
Born down by wind or age or snow,
Had not another neighbor tree
Held out its arms in sympathy.
Shall trees be nobler to their kind
Than men, who boast the noble mind;
Shall there exist within the wood
This great eternal brotherhood
Of oak and pine, of hill and fen,
And not within the hearts of men?
God grant that men are like to these
And brothers brotherly as trees.

—Author Unknown.

II

Mutual Aid is a Fundamental Principle of Nature

"Go to the ant thou sluggard, consider her ways and be wise." Proverbs 6:6.

Learning From Nature

The above verse from Proverbs suggests something which writers of the Old and New Testament frequently observed, namely, learning lessons of life from the realm of nature. Jesus often taught great lessons by pointing to situations in nature from which men could learn valuable truths. It is, therefore, proper in a discussion of the subject of mutual aid to draw some lessons from the kingdom of nature which is just as truly God's creation as is man himself.

It is fascinating to discover the wide variety of species in the animal kingdom that practice the law of mutual aid instead of a rugged and ruthless law of competition. Mutual aid is not something taught animals by man. It is a God-given gift, implanted as a very instinct into their lives. It is necessary to emphasize this fact because since the days of Charles Darwin and Herbert Spencer, there has been so much emphasis on the doctrine of the survival of the fittest and on the laws of competition that a great many people have come to believe that only ruthless competition characterizes the laws of nature. This is an error, because cooperation is quite as important a factor in the natural world as is competition.

There is no denial that there is struggle and competition for food and for dominance between animal species, but it must also be remembered that along with this element of struggle is the element of mutual assistance. These two tendencies exist side by side. Warder C. Allee, an eminent American zoologist, claims that there is a kind of unconscious mutuality or cooperation practiced among animals from the highest all the way down to the lowest forms of plant and animal life. The difference in the practice of mutual aid is more a matter of degree than of kind. All species practice a form of it but some species practice it in a much more thorough going fashion than others.

The Ant

One of the most widely recognized and most popular illustrations of mutual aid among animals is that found in the life of ants. Kropotkin gives us a vivid description of that phase of ant life which demonstrates this point.

If we take an ant's nest, we not only see that every description of work, rearing of progeny, foraging, building, rearing of aphides, and so on is performed according to the principles of voluntary mutual aid. We must also recognize . . . that the fundamental feature of life of many species of ants is in the fact and obligation for sharing its food, even though already swallowed and partly digested, with every member of the community which may apply for it . . . If one of them is hungry or thirsty and . . . the other has its crop full, it immediately asks for food; the individual thus requested never refuses, it sets apart its mandibles, takes a proper position, and regurgitates a drop of transparent fluid which is licked up by the hungry ant . . . If an ant which has its crop full has been selfish enough to refuse feeding a comrade, it will be treated as an enemy or even worse.[1]

Birds

Another evidence of the mutual dependence and common effort in wild life is manifested among those birds that annually migrate. Here we see that birds which have scattered in small flocks over a wide territory during the mating and nesting season congregate at a given place before they start on their migration. After waiting for several days for the late-comers to arrive, they finally start their mass flight in a certain well-chosen direction—the fruit of accumulated collective experience.[2]

---

[1] Prince Kropotkin, *Mutual Aid a Factor in Evolution* (New York: McClure, Phillips and Co., 1902), Introduction, p. 12. This volume is a classic in its field. It was written to combat the widely accepted Darwin theory of the survival of the fittest. Kropotkin says: "We have heard so much lately of the 'harsh, pitiless struggle for life,' which was said to be carried on by every animal against all other animals, every 'savage' against all other 'savages,' and every civilized man against all his co-citizens—and these assertions have so much become an article of faith—that it was necessary, first of all, to oppose to them a wide series of facts showing animal and human life under quite a different aspect."

[2] *Ibid.*, p. 36.

It has frequently been observed that large and small birds sometimes band together for migratory flight. It appears that the large birds serve in the capacity of protectors for the small ones. One naturalist has reported seeing on several occasions a party of cranes which had a flock of larks flying in the middle and on both sides of their migratory columns.[1]

Beavers

Among the larger animals, such as beaver, the social life and daily practice of mutual helpfulness are quite well known. Beavers live in colonies and work together to accomplish their common tasks with such a high degree of cooperation that their method and achievement might justly be envied and profitably imitated by man. Other animals which live naturally in social groups and practice mutual aid include the deer, buffalo, wild goats, sheep, wolves and horses.

Horses

Horses that roam the plains in packs before they are tamed, illustrate the necessity of practicing mutual aid as a method of survival. Kropotkin describes the wild horses of Siberia as follows:

> When a beast of prey approaches them, several studs unite at once; they repulse the beast and sometimes chase it, and neither the wolf nor the bear, not even the lion can capture a horse or even a zebra as long as they are not detached from the herd ... When a snow storm rages in the steppes, each stud keeps close together and goes to a protected ravine. But if confidence disappears or the group has been seized by panic and disperses, the horses perish and the survivors are found after the storm half dying from fatigue. Union is their chief arm in the struggle for life, ...[2]

An interesting aspect of the psychological value of mutual aid is here demonstrated. Unless the horses retain confidence in each other and remain united, they are lost, whether the foe is another species of animal or a threat from a natural force such as a storm.

---

[1] *Ibid.*
[2] *Ibid.*, p. 46ff.

Adaptation

A fundamental lesson that we may learn from nature is that where mutual aid is not possible, adaptation is a preferable alternative to competition. By means of adaptation either to the natural elements, to other species or to the type of food, competition is either eliminated or greatly reduced. In this way the struggles in life may still yield the greatest fullness and intensity with the least waste of energy. The lesson of adaptation is illustrated in the numerous customs of animal life as described by Kropotkin:

> Most of the birds slowly move southward as the winter comes, or gather in numberless societies and undertake long journeys—and thus avoid competition. Many rodents fall asleep when the time comes that competition should set in; while other rodents store food for the winter, and gather in large villages for obtaining the necessary protection when at work. The reindeer, when the lichens are dry in the interior of the continent, migrate towards the sea. Buffaloes cross an immense continent in order to find plenty of food. And the beavers, when they grow numerous on a river, divide into two parties and go, the old ones down the river; the young ones up the river—and avoid competition. And when animals can neither fall asleep nor migrate, nor lay in stores, nor themselves grow their food like the ants, they do what the titmouse does . . . they resort to new kinds of food— and thus avoid competition.[1]

The lesson we are to learn from nature is that struggle and competition are to be avoided whenever possible. The lesson of adaptation is peculiarly appropriate for historic peace churches with their emphasis on non-resistance. They have believed it better to suffer than to inflict suffering. They have taught the wisdom of turning the other cheek or going the second mile and being exploited rather than exploit. They, like some animals, have chosen to migrate rather than carry on ruthless struggle and violent competition.

This brief discussion on mutual aid and the lessons to be learned from the natural world should remind us that the practice of mutual aid is deeply rooted in the behaviour of God's own creation. It is as though the Creator through the

---

[1] *Ibid.*, p. 74

space of time had meant to show that more could be accomplished by working together in groups than by working selfishly as individuals.

Mutual Aid Among Primitive People

In recent years, scholars have made many detailed studies of the customs, habits, and life of primitive peoples who are untouched by modern culture and modern standards of living. Primitive people live very close to nature. Among the more recent and more interesting studies of primitive peoples is that of Margaret Mead. In her book, *Cooperation and Competition Among Primitive Peoples*, she says after studying thirteen South Sea Island communities that three could be classified as competitive, six cooperative and four individualistic. She found that there is a relatively high degree of cooperation among members within each group, even if not between members of different tribes. Kropotkin said that mutual aid and support are such inherent parts of human nature that at no time in history could he discover men living in small isolated families, fighting each other for means of subsistence. Ralph Linton, Anthropologist, describes life among primitive people in Madagascar as follows:

> The conditions under which the Tanala live make it highly advantageous for a number of men to work together as a cooperative unit. Their main crop is rice, cultivated by the cutting and burning method. The jungle can be cleared more efficiently by gang labor than by single individuals. Moreover, gangs of men were in better position to repel enemy attacks, which were common prior to the beginning of French domination. Fifteen or twenty men working together can get a greater individual return for their labor than can the same number working separately, and this fact seems to have been important in establishing the joint family pattern . . . the habits of cooperation developed during the original father's domination are usually so strong that the family continues to function smoothly and efficiently under the eldest son's control.[1]

---

[1] Ralph Linton, *The Study of Man* (New York: Appleton-Century Co., 1936), pp. 190-91.

FUNDAMENTAL PRINCIPLE OF NATURE

If, therefore, primitive people who live in spiritual darkness practice mutual aid and show consideration and concern for one another, how much more should reborn Christians do so. Even though we claim to be highly civilized and though we claim to possess much knowledge, we should not be above learning from God through the realm of nature.

SUGGESTIONS:

1. Study carefully certain insect, bird or animal habits to see if you can observe evidences of mutual aid.

2. List examples from your reading or observations that illustrate the deep-rooted nature of mutual aid in natural life.

QUESTIONS:

1. What evidence is there in the life cycle of flowers, plants and trees that there is an element of mutual dependency?

2. Was the world as God created it originally intended to practice mutual aid?

3. Is there any evidence in the first chapter of Genesis that mutual aid is one of the laws of the universe?

4. Are we competitive by nature or do we learn to be competitive through our customs, our teachings and our cultural environment?

5. What lessons in mutual aid have you learned from insects, birds or animals?

III

The Bible and Mutual Aid

"They shall sit every man under his own vine and under his fig tree and none shall make them afraid." Micah 4:4.

When we look for evidences of mutual aid in the Old Testament, we are rewarded with abundant illustrations. It is well to remember that Hebrew society in Old Testament times was strongly dependent upon the kinship institutions of the family, the clan and the tribe. These institutions were the center of Jewish life. Primary attention was paid to the family and the tribe rather than to the individual. This accounts, in part, for the many evidences of mutual aid among the Hebrew people. Religion, government and economics were all intimately related.

The customs and traditions of the Hebrews in Bible times would have forbidden the extremely individualistic practices and theories commonly found among Jews and Christians in our own day. The homes of individual families were not scattered in isolated units over the Palestine countryside but were clustered in small villages. This was necessary in part as a protective measure against dangers from without. Newly conquered territories were held as common property and divided by lot among all the members of the community. (Micah 2:4, 5; Deut. 12:12; Josh. 14:4; Jer. 32:7). It has been suggested that the arrangement of the Sabbatic Year is a carryover from the earlier communal landholding policy. The ancient Hebrew society was a form of social organization that was cooperative by nature.

Mutual Aid in the Old Testament

The flight of the Children of Israel from Egypt is one long story of mutual aid. If it had not been for the united efforts of the Israelities, they would never have been able to complete their exodus. In fact, whenever the mutual efforts of the group were threatened by internal dissension and the refusal to cooperate, the success of the entire migration was threatened.

It was only by means of sharing hardships and working together that morale was maintained and ultimate success achieved. (Read Exodus, Chapters 13-20.)

The building of the walls around Jerusalem under the leadership of Nehemiah is an illustration of mutual aid on a large scale. Here, too, in spite of opposition and ridicule, it was only because of determination and cooperation that the huge task was completed. (Neh. Chapters 2-6).

The vigorous struggle of the prophets for social justice was an attack on selfishness and sin and an attempt to call the children of Israel's attention to their obligations to each other and to God. It was an effort, too, to develop responsibility within the Israelitish family for sharing duties, hardships, joys and material accumulations. It was not presented as a matter of choice but rather as a demand of God. Cooperative practices that had formerly been confined to the immediate family were now to be extended to the entire Hebrew nation which came to be regarded as a single religious clan or brotherhood.

In the Book of Deuteronomy, we find that the owner of a vineyard had to allow a poor man the right to eat as many grapes as he cared for while working in the vineyard, although the hired man was not permitted to carry any away with him. (Deut. 23:25). The tenth part of the yield of every third year was to be kept for the members in the brotherhood who needed it, such as the poor, the widows, the orphans and the strangers. (Deut. 14:28). In Deut. 22:1-4 the laws of the brotherhood were further outlined in these words:

> You must not see your fellow countryman's ox or sheep go astray without showing concern for it; you must be sure to take it home to your fellow countryman. If, however, your fellow countryman is not a tribesman of yours and you do not know him, you must take it home with you, and keep it until your fellow countryman claims it: then you must give it back to him. You must do the same with his ass, with his garment, and anything lost by a fellow countryman of yours, which he has lost and you have found; you are not to be without concern for it . . .
> (Goodspeed Translation)

We see here a sense of responsibility for assistance to men beyond the boundaries of the tribe or race. Hebrew religion had risen to a high ethical plane. In the mind of the Hebrews, mutual concern for each other's welfare was considered the will of God.

Mutual Aid in the New Testament

The emphasis of Jesus' teaching was on the general principle of Christian brotherhood. Emphasis on mutual aid, therefore, is implied rather than specifically stated. When Jesus instructs his disciples to go forth, he tells them they are not to be burdened with such material matters as money, extra clothing or food. He assures them that those to whom they will preach will provide for their needs. (Matt. 10:8ff). The principle of mutual aid is very clearly enunciated by Jesus in the parable of the Good Samaritan when he defined the meaning of neighbor to the young lawyer who sought the way to eternal life.

The principle of mutual aid in the New Testament is perhaps best expressed in the Book of Acts. The principle can be summarized as "each according to ability and each according to his need." In Acts 4:35 we are told that "distribution was made unto every man according as he had need." The same thought is expressed in Acts 2:45, and we are told further that those who believed continued daily with one accord in the temple and breaking bread from house to house did eat their meat with gladness and singleness of heart. It can be assumed that this joy was the result of genuine fellowship one with another in Christ.

Paul on Mutual Aid

In the writings of Paul, we see how some of the early Christians carried out Jesus' teachings and how his efforts resulted in the establishment of flourishing Christian fellowships. Wherever churches were established, mutual aid became the accepted way of doing things. In Acts 20:35 Paul mentions how he has always worked with his hands to support himself and his companions yet he points out that Christians should be concerned with people other than themselves.

In writing to the Romans, Paul emphasizes Jesus' teachings of the Sermon on the Mount and tells his fellow Christians to supply the needs of God's people. In Romans 13:8 he says: "Owe nobody anything except the duty of mutual love." In Romans 15:1-2 he says that it is the duty of those who are strong to put up with the handicaps of those who are weak and that we ought not to seek to please ourselves only but to do good to our neighbor and help in his development. In

Romans 16:2, in introducing Phoebe, Paul says: "Give her whatever help she may need from you for she has herself been a protection and a blessing to many, including myself." In Philippians 2:4 we are told: "Do not take account of your own interests, but of the interests of others as well. Have the same attitude that Christ Jesus had."

Paul's famous comparison of the Church with the human body emphasizes that each part is necessary for every other part and that it is important for all parts to work mutually together. This is further evidence of how important the practice of mutual aid appeared in the eyes of the early Christians. In the second epistle to the Corinthians, 8:12-14, Paul says: "If a man is willing to give, the value of his gift is in porportion to what he has not. I do not mean to be easy upon others, and hard upon you, but to equalize the burden and in the present situation to have your plenty make up for what they need so that some day their plenty may make up for what you need . . ." Here Paul clearly sees the nature of genuine Christian mutual aid. This is an injunction for one group of believers to help another group so that if conditions are reversed, mutual aid might still work effectively.

In Ephesians 4:28 Paul says: ". . . the man who stole must not steal anymore, he must work with his hands at honest toil instead so as to have something to share with those in need." The implication is clear that the very purpose of a man's work is to produce so as to have something to share with his brethren. The correction for dishonesty here is also interesting in that it implies that honest work and the joy of sharing the fruits of one's labor remove temptations to dishonesty. To the Galatians, Paul makes it very specific that they are to "Bear one another's burdens and so fulfill the law of Christ." (Gal. 6:2). The second part of this admonition is an important commentary, namely that bearing one another's burdens is the law of Christ.

Mutual Aid in the Epistles

All of the New Testament writers stress the practice of mutual aid among Christians. Some of them expressed themselves even stronger than Paul did. For instance, in the first Epistle of John 3:17, we are asked: "If anyone who is rich sees his brother in need and closes his heart against him, how can he have love for God in his heart?" A little later in the

Epistle, the writer appeals for a concrete expression of love; one that goes beyond a mere verbal profession: "Let us not love with words and lips only but in reality and truth." In the third Epistle of John, there are beautifully appropriate words of admonition regarding the responsibility of Christian brothers for each other. These words might well apply to the Mennonite Church and her treatment of members who have or will return from giving years of service on the relief field or in C.P.S.: "Which have borne witness of thy charity before the Church; . . . because that for his name's sake they went forth, taking nothing of the Gentiles. We, therefore, ought to receive such that we might be fellow-helpers to the truth." (III John 1:6-8). James is even more vigorous in his plea that love should express itself in fruitful work within the brotherhood. He says:

> My brothers, what is the good of a man's saying he has faith, if he has no good deed to show? Can faith save him? If some brother or sister has no clothes and has not food enough for a day, and one of you says to them, 'Goodbye, keep warm and have plenty to eat,' without giving them the necessaries of life, what good does it do? . . . (James 2:14-17).

Pagans Testimony to Christian Mutual Aid

It is interesting to note how impressive to the pagans of that time was the practice of mutual aid among the early Christians. The ancient Latin writer, Lucian, who was not a Christian, tells in a satirical way the story of an early Christian hero by the name of Peregrine who was imprisoned. In the following words he describes aid which Christians rendered to their imprisoned brother:

> The Christians took it all very seriously; he was no sooner in prison, than they began trying every means to get him out again—but without success. Everything else that could be done for him they most devoutly did. They thought of nothing else . . . Their officials bribed the gaolers to let them sleep inside with him. Elegant dinners were conveyed in; their sacred writings were read . . . In some of the Asiatic cities, too, the Christian communities put themselves to the expense of sending deputations, with offers of sympathy, assistance and legal advice. The activity of these people, in dealing with any matter that

affects the community is something extraordinary; they spare no trouble, no expense.[1]

Lucian then explained to his pagan readers why the Christians did this. He says:

You see, these misguided creatures start with the general conviction that they are immortal for all time, which explains the contempt of death and voluntary self-devotion which are common among them; and then it was impressed on them by their original lawgiver that they are all brothers, from the moment that they are converted, and deny the Gods of Greece, and worship the Crucified Sage, and live after his laws. All this they take quite on trust, with the result that they despise all worldly goods alike, regarding them merely as common property.[2]

From this evidence we see further proof that substantiates and elaborates what has been shown throughout the New Testament literature. Mutual aid is clearly taught and practiced by the early Christians in almost every walk of life. Interesting to the point of being thrilling is the characteristic spontaneousness and enthusiasm with which this mutual aid within the brotherhood was carried on. So devoted and sincere were many of the early believers that their sharing frequently resulted in communal ownership of goods. Believers aided one another with material substance, but they did more than that; they gave encouragement and sympathy through prayers, reading of the Scriptures, as well as sharing food and shelter.

The effect of this kind of mutual aid is well described by a student of life among the early Christians who says that:

Within the circle of disciples, the love which Jesus inculcated burned warm and vivid, and one of the most characteristic marks of the life of his followers in the apostolic age was their devotion to one another and their unselfish regard for each other's good. It was this thing more than anything else that gave its peculiar character to their Christian life, and it did much to attract others to them.[3]

It must be abundantly clear, therefore, that mutual aid is a principle thoroughly established in the Christian religion

---
[1] The works of Lucian of Samosata translated by H. W. Fowler and F. G. Fowler, (Oxford, Claremdon Press, 1905), Vol. IV, p. 82.
[2] Ibid. p. 83.
[3] A. C. McGiffert, *A History of Christianity in the Apostolic Age*, (New York; Scribners, 1900).

with its roots deep in the history of Judaism. As in so many other things, Christ exalted and enriched this aspect of Christian brotherhood. One cannot measure the effectiveness of mutual aid as an aspect of the total Christian witness but one may assume that it is an inevitable consequence of genuine rebirth in Christ and as such must be emphasized not only among individuals but among groups of reborn believers as was the case among the first century Christians. James Moffat states that on the whole, the most common and effective Christian propaganda during the first two or three centuries was that the Christians lived their religion as well as talked about it.

SUGGESTIONS:

1. Make a list of illustrations that demonstrate the practice of mutual aid in one of the Gospels; one of Paul's letters; one of the epistles.

2. See if you can find additional evidences that Christians influenced pagans by their acts of Christian brotherliness.

QUESTIONS:

1. What examples are there of mutual aid in connection with the exodus of the Israelites from Egypt?

2. Does the story of Joseph teach a lesson on mutual aid?

3. What evidence is there that the early Christians demonstrated as well as taught brotherliness?

4. Does the Third Epistle of John have any suggestion that throws light on whether CPS men should have been paid wages by the Government?

5. Do you know of people today who have been attracted to Christ because of the love and brotherhood that was manifested by church people in your community?

IV

Our Forefathers Believed in Mutual Aid

"Be not conformed to this world: but be ye transformed by the renewing of your mind." Romans 12:2.

We need to remind ourselves frequently of the general economic and social conditions that existed at the time the Mennonite Church was founded. To understand conditions then is to be able to appreciate more fully the reasons for holding the kind of faith our fathers held and for trying to develop the kind of a Christian fellowship they sought to establish.

During the sixteenth century, as in our own day, many people were thoroughly dissatisfied with the state of things in the church as well as in society in general. The Catholic Church had grown rich, powerful and corrupt. There was a sharp contrast between it and the plain religious teachings and practices of the New Testament Christians. Socially, society was divided into three classes: the clergy, the nobility and the common peasantry. The first two were the ruling classes in the religious and political spheres. Socially, these two classes were the aristocracy, and economically they were the wealthy. The duty of the peasantry was to labor for the material support of the two privileged classes in the capacity of farmers, craftsmen and small traders.

Our Fathers Were Peasants and Craftsmen

The lot of the common man was economically and socially oppressive. On top of this was the revolting condition within the Catholic Church. The worldly life of the clergy with the comforts and ease that the accumulation of wealth permitted, the enjoyment and abuse of power and privileges and the lack of piety and evangelical zeal, all turned the more devout souls against the existing church.

Some of the more courageous and daring individuals decided to break with things as they were and launch on a new path. The courage of Luther had opened the flood gates and after him came a host of fellow reformers. The Anabaptists, however, did not stop where Luther did. He wanted only to reform the Catholic Church, but they wanted to establish a new church on the pattern of New Testament Christianity. The church they established was a believer's church—it was a communion of saints; a fellowship; a brotherhood of the reborn.

What our fathers tried to do was to bring spiritually reborn men and women together into a Christian fellowship where members would encourage one another to live lives of purity, holiness and complete obedience to God's will. Menno Simons described the fellowship as one "without spot or wrinkle." This meant that the Holy Spirit which was manifested in Jesus Christ would have to dwell in the hearts of all church members. The relationship of one to another was to be as brother to brother and sister to sister with God as the loving Father. The chief aim of the Anabaptists was to establish a pure Christian brotherhood; a community of the spirit where the love of God was the chief factor in motivating all action and determining all conduct. This having been the conception of what characterized the true body of believers, we can readily understand why our forefathers believed in mutual aid.

Mutual Aid A Custom

Because of the medieval structure of society in which our early forefathers lived, they practiced mutual aid in much of their daily life even before they established a new church. This was true because as members of the peasantry, they found it economically advantageous and socially desirable to do so. Farmers and craftsmen of the 16th century lived in village communities. Mutual efforts were necessary in order to make effective demands against their superiors who commonly exploited them. Socially, too, mutual efforts were a way of lightening the burdens of a hard life. Cooperative labor was often necessary in plowing and harvesting because no single villager had the material resources to carry on these activities alone. It often required all the available oxen from several families in a village to draw a single plow or a wagon. At harvest time men, women and children all turned to the fields to assist one another in a common activity.

It was the custom, too, for farmers to own certain lands in common such as the pasture, the meadow, the woods and the waste. Mutual aid expressed by farmers under these conditions was characterized by its informal and spontaneous nature. There were no written agreements or formal organizations created to carry out such mutual activity—nor, was there need for any since the village was small and all members were intimately acquainted with each other and contacts outside the immediate neighborhood were few. Mutual aid, therefore, was very much a part of tradition and custom.

Views on Mutual Aid

Among the Anabaptists were those who believed that true Christianity required the believers to share all earthly possessions in common and thus the church for them became a genuine communal brotherhood. This group has as its direct descendants, the Hutterite Brethren who exist today in South Dakota, Montana, and various provinces in Canada, England and Paraguay.

Those Anabaptists who did not share the convictions of the communal minded ones might be called semi-communal Anabaptists. They believed that followers of Christ should live in communities with the responsibility of administering God's possessions. Those who held this view believed it proper for individuals to own private property so long as it was used to the glory of God and the common good rather than for the sake of gratifying their personal selfishness and vanity.

It is very clear that in the thinking of our Anabaptist forefathers, human rights were given precedence over property rights. Sharing of material good according to those who needed it was the accepted practice. This point is clearly emphasized in almost all the scattered writings of those who spoke for the Anabaptists.

Hans Leopold, a minister of the Swiss Brethren Church in Augsburg, and one who suffered martyrdom in 1528, said that, "If they know of anyone who is in need, whether or not he is a member of their church, they believe it their duty out of love to God, to render him help and aid."[1] Heinrich Seiler who was drowned in 1536 at Bern, Switzerland, said: "I do not believe it is wrong that a Christian has property of his own, provided he will do right and share his goods with the needy, for he is nothing more than a steward."[2]

---
[1] John Horsch, "The Faith of the Swiss Brethren," Mennonite Quarterly Review, Vol. V (1931) p. 139, quoted from J. Kuhn, *Toleranz und Offenbarung*, p. 281.
[2] Ibid. (quoting Muller, Bernische Taufer, p. 44).

An early Hutterian source claims that among the Swiss Anabaptists it was the practice to administer baptism only to those who vowed to "consecrate themselves with all their temporal possessions to the service of God and His people."[1] In the Swiss Brethren Congregation at Strassburg in Alsace (1557) applicants for membership were asked whether they were willing to devote all their possessions to the church and its needs, if necessity required, and not to fail any member that was in need, if they were able to render aid.[2]

Heinrich Bullinger says that according to the Swiss Brethren teaching "every good Christian is under duty before God to use from motives of love all his possessions to supply the necessities of life to any of his brethren."[3] It should be pointed out that Bullinger was an enemy of the Swiss Brethren; therefore, such a statement would certainly not be prejudiced in their favor. A contemporary writer says concerning the Swiss Brethren in Augsburg that "in their brotherhood there was in evidence the purpose to render each other the greatest possible help from motives of brotherly love"[4]

These few quotations illustrate beyond a doubt that the early Swiss Brethren had a keen concern for the economic and social welfare of their own members and, on several known occasions, for people outside their own brotherhood.

The Brethren practiced mutual aid so genuinely that they were frequently accused of being religious communists even though they, themselves, believed in and practiced private ownership of goods.

In a disputation at Frankenthal in 1571, when one of the brethren was accused of being a communist, he, acting as spokesman for the group replied, "We confess that Christians may have private property without violating Christian love, always with the provision that they do not misuse it but at all times let their abundance serve the needs of the poor, as Paul teaches in II Cor. 8:10-15."[5]

Balthasar Hubmaier, one of the outstanding leaders of the Brethren, says in his answer to a charge of being a communist that he never held to community of goods. He declared himself in favor of the kind of community of goods that he

---
[1] Ibid. (quoting from *Verant wortung den Schweizern getan auf ihr Begheren*).
[2] Ibid. (quoting Falshof. *Doopsge zinden te Straatsburg*, p. 214).
[3] Ibid. (quoting from Bullinger. *Wider Touffern ursprung*, fol. 129b).
[4] Ibid. (quoting from Meyer. "Widertaufer in Schwaben," *Zeitschrift Fur Kirchengeschichte*, XVIII (1897) p. 252).
[5] Ibid. (quoting from *Protocoll Framckenthol*, p. 533).

believed the early Christians in the Jerusalem community practiced. This, he thought, was to the effect that Christian believers should hold property subject to the needs of the brotherhood. All of the Anabaptists inculcated the duty of sharing and stressed the claims of the less well-to-do on the more well-to-do members of the community.

In a public debate with Martin Bucer, a man by the name of Schnabel speaking for the Anabaptist Brethren states his reason for leaving the Lutheran State Church.[1] He says that he had been in charge of the treasury for the poor in the Lutheran Church, but noticed that the management of the funds was not carried out in the biblical spirit. He complained to the pastor about the custom of loaning out church money on interest while many of the poor in the community were in great need. For this reason he told the pastor, the mayor and the council of Marburg that his conscience compelled him to separate from the state church and become an Anabaptist. It appears that the Anabaptist practice of accepting responsibility for the needs of their members and the habit of making money available to the needy without interest attracted this man to them.

Mutual Aid Among the Early Dutch Fathers

What has been said about the Swiss Brethren is equally characteristic of the Dutch Anabaptists from whom came Menno Simons and that long list of worthy Christian descendants who moved eastward to Prussia and Russia and later westward to United States, Canada, Paraguay, Brazil and Mexico.

Menno Simons in his "Appeal to the Common People" spoke clearly of the matter of responsibility for mutual welfare in the brotherhood. He said, "We are ready before God and man, with all our hearts, to bestow our possessions, gold and all that we have, however little it may be, and in addition thereunto our sweat and labor, to meet the necessities of the poor, as the Spirit and the Word of the Lord and true brotherly love teach us."[2] In the same article he says: "He who delights in the Word of the Lord speaks the truth from the heart, crucifies his flesh and will give his goods and blood for the Word of the Lord, if it be required."[3]

[1] Christian Hege, "The Early Anabaptists in Hesse," *MQR*, Vol. V (1931). p. 167.
[2] Menno Simons, "Appeal to The Common People," *Complete Works of Menno Simons*, Part I (Elkhart, John F. Funk & Bro., 1871) p. 83.
[3] *Ibid.*

It is characteristic of Menno in most of his writings to refer to both the Word and the Spirit of the Lord. Menno did not separate religion from the social and economic aspects of life, but rather emphasized their inter-relationship. Faith is always stressed, but only as it is demonstrated in concrete life situations. A Dutch author in 1698 wrote as follows:

> We may learn much that is good from these people, namely: humility, contentment, moderation, and especially mercy toward the needy. For although the people of the Reformed Church of Holland deserve to be commended for their benevolence toward the poor, yet this virtue is particularly true of these people. Also, they are very careful to dress unassumingly.[1]

Intercession For Brethren in Distress

Concern for Brethren in other countries was manifested on a number of occasions by our Mennonite forefathers. When Mennonites in Switzerland were oppressed and in bondage as galley slaves, the Dutch Mennonites asked their Government to intercede for their Swiss Brethren by appealing to the Swiss Government for leniency and release. Correspondence between the Burgomaster of Amsterdam and the Burgomaster and the Council of Bern, Switzerland is still in existence. At another time, the Dutch officials at Amsterdam succeeded in getting King William III of England to intercede in behalf of the oppressed Mennonites in the Palatinate. The king wrote to Duke William and persuaded him to treat the Mennonites in question more civilly. This effort initiated by the Dutch Mennonites halted persecution and resulted in the restoration of confiscated property. In addition, the Mennonites were given the right to engage in business and trade.

It is reported that as early as 1630, it was the custom of Mennonites to provide land for those among their number who needed it as a means of earning a living. The aid given was the kind which was intended to improve the economic and social condition of the recipient. It was aid that was intended to help members to become self-supporting.

During the eighteenth century, economic and political conditions in Europe compelled thousands of Mennonites to mi-

---

[1] Horsch, "The Character of the Evangelical Anabaptists as Reported by Contemporary Reformation Writers," *MQR*, VIII (July, 1934), 167.

grate. From Germany and from Switzerland, Mennonite immigrants streamed to America, while significant numbers of them moved eastward from Prussia to Russia. The Dutch Aid Fund was administered by the Committee for Foreign Needs. Over 50,000 guilders were raised for the purpose of assisting the migrants. As the money was paid back by those benefited, it was placed in a revolving fund and became available again for others.

In Germany, before the principle of non-resistance was given up by the Mennonites, it was customary for all members to share in the raising of the required exemption money which Mennonites had to pay as a fine for refusing military service. It is significant that while most Dutch Mennonites abandoned the principle of non-resistance, they still kept alive a tender conscience on the matter of mutual aid for deserving members of the brotherhood.

Mutual Aid Outside the Brotherhood

Mutual Aid rendered by the Mennonites of Europe was not entirely confined to their own group. In a letter written by the Walloon Mennonite Church to the Mennonite Church in Bern in 1660, among other things is mentioned the help rendered the Waldenses who were undergoing great persecution in the Piedmont Valley in Italy. The Dutch Mennonites also extended assistance to the French Huguenots after the revocation of the Edict of Nantes. Even during the recent crisis of the Jews in Germany, the Dutch Mennonites provided financial assistance and shelter in their Brotherhood retreat grounds for Jewish refugees.

In the light of the present-day cooperation between Friends and Mennonites administering the Civilian Public Service program, it is also interesting to note the friendly relations existing between English Quakers and the Dutch and German Mennonites early in the eighteenth century. In fact, the Dutch Mennonites and English Quakers have maintained close contact up to the present time. It has been customary for representatives from each group to attend each other's meetings. Robert Barkley makes frequent references to the hospitality extended to Quakers traveling among the Mennonites on the Continent. He refers to one instance where the Friends at a yearly meeting in 1709 contributed fifty pounds to the Palatinate Mennonites who had fled from Calvinist persecution in Switzerland.

Mutual aid as expressed in the foregoing cases seems to have been motivated by genuine Christian love. It was not the result of a secular teaching of economic equality, but it was rather the result of a New Testament emphasis that assistance should be rendered by each according to his ability and to each according to his need. Genuine Christian brotherliness was stressed and earnestly sought, but there is no evidence of a desire to have all men reduced to a common economic level.

SUGGESTIONS:

1. To understand the origin of the Mennonite Church, read about social and religious conditions in Reformation times. Several excellent references are two books by James Westfall Thompson, *Economic and Social History of the Middle Ages*, New York: Century Co. 1928, and *The Later Middle Ages* published by the same company in 1931—both books are authoritative and very thorough. Thomas Lindsay, *A History of the Reformation*, Vol. II, New York: Scribner, 1907 is a very delightful and factual book approaching the subject from the view of a church historian. See also John Horsch, *Mennonites in Europe*, Mennonite Publishing House, Scottdale, Pennsylvania, 1942.

QUESTIONS:

1. What kind of a church were our forefathers trying to build?

2. What were the Anabaptist views toward ownership of private property by Christians?

3. On what authority did our forefathers base mutual aid?

4. How are social and economic views of our early forefathers practical or impractical today?

5. Was the practice of mutual aid confined to membership within the Mennonite Brotherhood?

V

Our Forefathers Practiced Mutual Aid

"For his name sake they went forth, taking nothing of the Gentiles." III John 7.

In addition to the voluntary and largely spontaneous forms of mutual activity carried on by our forefathers, there were also more systematic and highly organized expressions of it. Among the European Mennonites, institutions were established for care of the aged, the sick and the orphaned. Many of these institutions are now several centuries old.

In Germany and Holland

In the Danzig Mennonite community there was a three hundred year old home for the aged which is now destroyed as a result of the present war. The Mennonites in Crefeld, Germany also established homes for their aged dependents. These institutions were supported by the entire community. The home for the aged at Crefeld was arranged on the order of a modern apartment house, where each aged couple or single person had the privacy of his own apartment. These arrangements enabled the aged, the sick and the orphaned to be looked after by the total brotherhood. It prevented such individuals from being cast out of the fellowship of friends and loved ones and at the same time made it unnecessary for indigent Mennonites to become charges of the local municipality or of governmental agencies.

Early records show that mutual insurance was practiced by Mennonites in the beginning of the 17th Century, and had its origin among Mennonites in Germany in 1623. Mennonites then living in the Province of West Prussia organized the "Tiegenhoefer Privat Brandordnung," (Private Fire Regulation of Tiegenhof) which association was still in existence up to World War II. It was operated for the protection of those people of the Mennonite faith who lived in that Province. Its offices were at Tiegenhof, West Prussia, Germany. In point of years, it is more than 100 years older than the first insurance company organized in America, which is the Philadelphia Contributionship founded by Benjamin Franklin in 1752.

The Dutch Mennonites in 1710 organized the General Committee for Foreign Needs. It has been in continuous existence ever since, rendering assistance wherever needed among various Mennonite groups at various times and places. A revolving fund was provided to give aid. Sometimes, the assistance was in the form of outright gifts and sometimes in the form of loans. As the money was paid back by those who had been benefited, it became available for others in need.

A second organization among the Dutch Mennonites known as the Dutch Mennonite Committee for Emigrants has rendered generous service from time to time. This committee rendered active assistance to the Mennonite refugees from Russia who settled in Brazil between 1930-1932. It helped the refugee Mennonites in Brazil finance the building of a starch factory, two sawmills, two flour mills and several stores. In addition, it furnished money for schools, for medical aid and one cow for each family.

In Russia

The Mennonites in Russia had a long list of mutual aid organizations and activities. Many of them were brought from Prussia and earlier from Holland; others were developed in their new homes in the land of the Czar. The mutual aid organizations and practices were important factors in the development of their unique culture.

The Mennonite settlements in Russia furnish an interesting illustration of the course Mennonitism may take where it is free to develop its religious principles without political or religious restrictions. In Russia for the first time in their history, Mennonites were absolutely at liberty to practice their religious and social principles, to expand their settlement, to master their arts and crafts, and to develop the kind of Christian community life they desired. All this they could do without restraint or interference by the political state or by a dominant state church. Their only restraints were against proselyting religiously and against inter-marrying with Russians. Mennonites grouped themselves into small agricultural villages after the typical European pattern. In the beginning everyone was a farmer, but as time went on, a number of commercial and industrial enterprises developed. Not all of

them were privately owned. C. Henry Smith gives a vivid description of some of the cooperatively owned enterprises:
While these colonies were not communistic in their organization, yet the villages frequently undertook municipal enterprises for the common good. Some villages had a common granary stored with grain for the benefit of lean years and tracts of land for later distribution as the population grew. In 1820, the municipal flock of the old colony (Chortitz) consisted of 1000 Merinos, while income from the municipal ferry across the Dnieper was from two to three thousand rubles annually. The municipal distillery also netted a substantial profit for the common treasury that year.[1]

Among the most significant mutual aid organizations in Russia was the "Waisenamt" (orphans' office). This organization is still a characteristic part of the lives of some of the Mennonites in Canada, Mexico and Paraguay. It was originally an organization designed to administer funds for orphans and widows, but in time it became something of a trust company. In addition to administering estates, it provided limited banking services such as receiving deposits and extending credit. The Waisenamt in many ways substituted for the commercial banks and trust companies so common in our own day.

Other organized expressions of mutual aid among our fathers in Russia were the common ownership of high grade male breeding stock; such as stallions, bulls and rams. Through this cooperative economic arrangement it was possible to improve the quality of livestock over a period of years to a very high degree. So successful were Mennonites as farmers and livestock breeders, that they served as models to the non-Mennonite communities in surrounding areas, as well as to Governmental officials. On occasions, the Czars Alexander I and Alexander II paid special visits to the Mennonite communities in the interest of observing their highly developed agricultural life. This development was due in part to the cooperative endeavors of the Mennonite people.

Land Settlement In Russia

One of the most far-sighted and useful expressions of mutual aid in Russia was the practice of establishing a Land Fund

---

[1] C. Henry Smith, *The Coming of the Russian Mennonites*, (Berne, Indiana: The Mennonite Book Concern, 1927) p. 34.

for the purpose of buying and settling new land. Periodically the question of overcrowding arose due to a natural population increase. When the land in one community was fully occupied it became necessary to provide additional places of settlement, otherwise, a growing landless class would develop. Also, the Mennonites had an agreement with the Russian Government not to divide their land into farms of less than 65 dessiatines or about 175 acres. Thus a father could not divide his farm among his children.

The Land Fund was built up by renting out the unsold land to colony members. The money thus accumulated provided a nucleus for the purchase of additional tracts of land. Large new tracts were purchased and laid out into family farm sites. All those interested in buying land in the new settlement could then do so. If parents were unable to finance their newly married son and daughter they were extended credit from the Community Fund. The conditions of repayment and the rate of interest, if any, were determined by the community. This plan assumed that the young people as well as the older members in need were to be given a start in life at the expense of the brotherhood. The land fund was a systematic way of providing for community needs through mutual efforts. It reflects the sense of social responsibility felt for every member of the Christian community.

The religious and moral tone of this social responsibility is expressed by one of those who for many years was a member of such a community.

If the children and their children's children were left to individually provide for themselves as best they could, they, having no means of their own to a start anywhere, would drift singly or at best in insignificant little groups into all directions of the wide world and finding no useful application of their bodily strength, sink there into lamentable wretchedness and misery . . . They would lose all their church connections and their rooting in Mennonitism and whereas their fathers and grandfathers would sit in churches and worship, they most likely would be in moral sloughs; if left to themselves, their proletarianism would be almost certain, but by way of mutual aid activities the situation could be met honorably and the young people would get a chance to become respectable citizens.[1]

---

[1] Personal letter from J. J. Hildebrand, Winnipeg, Manitoba—1938.

OUR FOREFATHERS PRACTICED 35

This plan of land settlement is still being used by the Mennonites in Mexico today.

In addition to the mutual activities already mentioned in Russia, there were fire insurance associations, mutual stock buying and breeding companies, hospitalization plans and agricultural and educational improvement societies.

Among the Mennonites in Russia in the course of 120 years, thirty-six daughter colonies were established from the four mother colonies. Each colony was composed of a number of villages, the average being 8.7, and each village had from ten to thirty families.[1]

The coming of the Russian Revolution threatened the existence of the Mennonite settlements and their religious culture, but even in the twentieth century, the strong grounding in mutual aid served as a bulwark against the secularizing and demoralizing influence of the Bolshevik revolution.[2] Numerous villages and families were broken up, scattered and mixed with a variety of non-Mennonite people, thus destroying the solidarity and stability of the Mennonite communities. To counteract this situation, the Mennonites organized an All-Mennonite agricultural cooperative society. This organization was primarily agricultural in nature, concerning itself chiefly with the production and improvement of seed and livestock. It was designed to provide services and also to protect the Mennonite settlements against constant attempts on the part of the Communists to collectinize them.

The cooperative organization known as the All-Mennonite Agricultural Union consisted of nineteen branch units with fifty-six sub-branches, and it had a membership of five thousand, nine hundred sixty-five family-farm units. C. F. Klassen states that 80% of all the Mennonite farms in Siberia, on the Volga, in Turkestan, in the Caucasus and in the Crimea were in this organization. All Mennonite colonies in Russia, except those in the Ukraine, were included. Those in the Ukraine were separately organized. While there were many shortcomings among the Mennonites in Russia from a social and a religious point of view, it is fairly evident that their religiously motivated mutual aid served as a strong cohesive agent and prevented rapid disintegration. It gave Mennonite

---
1 *Die Mennoniten—Gemeiden in Russland*, 1914 bis 1920, Kommissions—Verlag der Mennon Fluchtlingsfursorge (1921) pp. 28-29.
2 C. F. Klassen, "The Mennonites of Russia, 1917-1928." *MQR*, Vol. VI (April, 1932) pp. 69-80.

culture in Russia much of its strength, stability and progressiveness.

In Colonial America

There are also illustrations of the practice of mutual aid in Colonial America, although this seems not to have been as highly developed in any formal sense as it was in Europe. Many of the old churches kept a record of such activities in their alms books. Unfortunately, few of these old books are still in existence. From the alms book of the Skippack Mennonites in Pennsylvania, it appears that this brotherhood frequently aided its needy members by extending loans to them without interest. For a number of years after 1831, Wenger reports that the annual statement declared that a certain individual had been loaned $300.00 without interest.[1] This was in keeping with the traditional Mennonite principle of opposition to charging interest.

There is another interesting demonstration of mutual aid in connection with the case of the Mennonites who migrated from eastern Pennsylvania to establish settlements in Waterloo County, Ontario. The early settlers in that county had purchased a large tract of land and discovered later that there was a heavy mortgage on it. Having used what little capital they had to purchase the land, they were unable to remove the mortgage and were, therefore, in danger of losing their entire investment. When the swindler was discovered, he attempted to clear himself by offering 60,000 acres of additional land at a ridiculously low price. The amount was 10,000 pounds. This, however, was more than the poor Mennonite pioneers could raise.

A delegation was sent to the Pennsylvania brothers in Lancaster County, Pennsylvania with the instructions to ask for help. After a thorough discussion of the plight of their brethren in Canada, it was agreed that help should be given, "not for the purpose of material gain, but as a brotherly act." A company was quickly formed and the money raised. In the spring of 1804, a wagon containing 20,000 solid silver dollars in cash was transported from Lancaster to Ontario as a first installment on the purchased land. A year later the balance was paid and title cleared.[2] Had it not been for this generous

---

[1] John C. Wenger, "The Alms Book of the Skippack Mennonite Church, 1738-1936," *MQR*, Vol. X, (April, 1936) p. 144.
[2] L. J. Burkholder, "The Early Mennonite Settlements in Ontario," *MQR*, Vol. III, (July, 1934), p. 118.

assistance of the Pennsylvania brethren, it would have meant certain financial loss for the victims of the swindle and possible failure of this settlement.

In Canada

Among the early Mennonite settlers in Canada, the practice of mutual aid was also common. C. A. Dawson describes the typical pattern in the following way:

In Manitoba, the Mennonites commenced farming with an equal distribution of land among all families. Villages were laid out by the central authorities. Usually from twenty to thirty congenial families took possession of each of these areas. During the period of pioneer economy, this form of settlement encouraged community cooperation in erecting barns, houses, mills, schools and churches. It promoted the loan and barter of animals, seed and farm equipment. Aid in times of distress was facilitated by the physical proximity of the pioneer villages. Common pastures and hayfields made for convenience and a saving of labor.[1]

It is quite evident in this brief discussion that mutual aid was practiced in a wide variety of ways by our forefathers. We have, therefore, a precedent for discussing the possibility of future developments of mutual aid among Mennonites.

SUGGESTIONS:

1. List as many additional illustrations of mutual aid as you can find in Mennonite history.

2. Find out how extensive is the mutual aid tradition in other churches, such as the Church of the Brethren, the Friends, the Lutherans, the Methodists, the Baptists.

QUESTIONS:

1. How old is the first known Mennonite mutual aid organization? For what purpose was it organized?

2. In what country did our forefathers develop mutual aid more extensively than anywhere else? Why?

3. What lessons can Mennonites of today learn from a study of mutual aid activities in the past?

4. What evidences of mutual aid were found among American Mennonites in colonial times?

5. Were mutual aid activities always confined to members of the Mennonite Church?

---

1 C. A. Dawson, *Group Settlements: Ethnic Communities in Western Canada*, (Toronto: MacMillan, 1936), p. 110.

VI

Mennonites Practice Mutual Aid Today

"But if any man provide not for his own, and especially for those of his own house, he hath denied the faith, and is worse than an infidel." I Timothy 5:8.

We have examined the attitudes and the practices of our forefathers on the question of mutual aid and have discovered certain rich traditions in our heritage. In addition to looking at the past, it is well to look around us and see what mutual aid enterprises are in evidence today. It is not our purpose in this pamphlet to give an exhaustive statistical list of mutual aid organizations and activities, but rather to indicate a variety of types of mutual enterprises found in various Mennonite communities throughout the world.

The United States

In the United States, Mennonites have developed mutual aid activities of two rather distinct types: one is of a strictly benevolent nature and consists of such institutions as hospitals, old peoples' homes and orphanages. There are approximately twenty-five old peoples' homes, fifteen hospitals and six orphanages conducted by Mennonites in the United States and Canada at the present time. All of them are supported by Mennonite people in the communities where they are located. Additional hospitals and old peoples' homes are being planned by Mennonites in various communities throughout the United States and Canada.

The second type of mutual aid is of a more strictly economic or business nature. It is difficult to draw the line clearly between benevolent and strictly economic types of mutual aid. Moving from the more strictly benevolent to the more economic types by degrees, we can mention first Mennonite mutual aid insurance societies, the most numerous being societies to insure against losses due to fire, storm, accident, hail, etc. The Mennonites of Virginia organized an automobile insurance society in 1934. It is the only one of its kind known to exist among Mennonites. There are over twenty Mennonite insurance societies in the United States alone, and an additional number of insurance societies among Mennonites in other countries. The majority of these societies were established as a result of religious motivation. This is illustrated in the preface of a pamphlet describing the rules and regulations of one such society, the Mennonite Aid Plan, whose headquarters are at Freeman, South Dakota.

> The action of our conference in 1882 in regard to the brotherhood assisting each other in cases of loss by fire, lightning, or storm has been met with general approval by most of the churches, both in the East and in the West, and we believe it will supply a long-felt want in the church in a manner that is entirely in accordance with the Word of God, without necessitating brethren to enter into the general insurance companies, against which many sincere brethren earnestly protest. We do not regard this plan as an insurance company, though it secures to the brethren who participate in it, the same benefits. It is simply a system through which the church is enabled more fully to carry out the apostolic admonition, 'Bear ye one another's burdens,' and to assist those who sustain losses from the causes mentioned above. We trust that this plan may be the means of good; that through its adoption no one may be weakened in his faith; but that on the contrary, the entire brotherhood may be encouraged to a deeper love and stronger sympathy for one another and to give cheerfully and systematically when losses occur, **so that when one brother suffers, all may suffer with him**, and so help to bear one another's burden.[1]

The Aid Plan insures all kinds of property for its members, such as houses, barns, crops, business houses, school houses (if they belong to Mennonites), saw mills, elevators, shops, engines, etc. It is of interest to note the spirit of brotherliness in which the Rules and Regulations of the Society are written. For instance, Articles 30 and 31:

> Each brother shall consider it his duty to warn his brother if he sees him negligent in taking proper precaution to guard against fire.

---

1 *Rules and Regulations of the Mennonite Aid Plan*: 1936.

As the views of the brethren in regard to the value of property differ, the brethren are requested, each one to act as his conscience dictates, to help bear one another's burden, and not to look on each other with suspicion, but to deal with one another as becometh Christians, in patience and charity.[1]

In another section of the by-laws, one finds the Mennonite principles asserted on moral matters when the society forbids the insuring of saloons, pool halls, moving pictures and "similar establishments with their contents." This illustrates the strong concern for brotherhood welfare and likewise the religious motivation lying behind the organization of Mennonite mutual aid.

It is a significant fact that practically all of the Mennonite insurance aid societies hold their annual meetings in churches and conduct their meetings somewhat on the order of a worship service, opening and closing each session with prayer and singing hymns at intervals throughout the meeting.

The Mennonite Aid Society, with headquarters at Mountain Lake, Minnesota, is in reality a life insurance company, although the term *life insurance* has always been avoided in favor of *aid society*. So far as is known, this is the only aid society that insures life, although there are a number of individual Mennonite congregations which have organized friendly societies for the purpose of giving modest financial assistance to members or their families at times of birth, marriage and death. The story of the Mennonite Aid Society at Mountain Lake, Minnesota and the purpose of its founding was told to the writer by one of the original members.

A group of men met in one of the stores one evening. We were discussing Mrs. R's plight. Her husband had dropped membership in a lodge at the request of his church. Soon after that, he died and left his widow without provision. This caused a discussion among the men assembled in the store that evening. Mr. H. P. Goertz pulled two dollars out of his pocket and said, 'I'll give this to the widow of the one of you who dies first if you will do the same.' Five or six of us agreed. Some others heard of it and likewise contributed until there were about 250 members. This was all unsolicited and unadvertised. We went to some of the ministers of the various churches and

---

[1] Ibid. p. 11.

asked that each church form an organization of this kind. They felt it would not be wise to do this as a church, but promised to join outside the church if one were organized. In about a year, an organization was formed and the membership continued to grow."[1]

This organization is purely mutual. Each member has one vote, and proxy voting by mail is permitted. A board of six directors is elected by the general membership, two each year at the annual meetings. The secretary-treasurer is the only member of the society receiving any remuneration for his work. As evidence of the fact that the society operates entirely for the benefit of its members we note that all of the assessment income goes for the payment of death benefits. The costs of operating the Society are defrayed entirely by the income from invested reserves. The maximum yearly assessment for over forty years has been twelve dollars. The membership totals approximately three thousand, of which all are Mennonites or adherents to Mennonite principles.

Cooperative Elevators

An increasing number of Mennonite communities have organized farmers cooperative elevators. These are especially common in Mennonite communities in Midwestern States and in the Prairie Provinces of Canada. We turn to Mountain Lake, Minnesota, for an illustration of the reason the farmers organized a cooperative elevator as well as for an interesting glimpse at the character of this business enterprise. In Mountain Lake, there are five Mennonite churches representing three branches of Mennonites. The elevator was organized, largely, through the personal initiative and persistence of Herman J. Fast. Farmers in the Mountain Lake community were being discriminated against in the prices that were being paid to them for feed and seed as over against the prices being paid to farmers in neighboring districts.

The repeated requests of the local farmers for relief from this discrimination were unheeded so the farmers succeeded in raising $3,500.00 to purchase a local elevator. This organization took effect in 1901 and has been efficiently operating ever since. A board of nine directors is elected at an annual meeting and profits are distributed to the members in proportion

---

[1] Personal Interview with I. I. Bargen, one of Mountain Lake's Pioneer leaders.

to the amount of their patronage. The purpose of the organization is to provide the farmers in the Mountain Lake region with a reliable agency through which to market grain and secure supplies of coal, feed, farm machinery and twine. Dividends have been paid to the members and interest has been paid regularly in all but two years of the company's history. Thus, the farmers by helping each other have earned for themselves thousands of dollars through the years. Mr. Fast, who was president of the Farmer's Cooperative Elevator for 37 years, explained the success of the cooperative in the following words:

> During all the years as president of this organization, there has never been a misunderstanding between members of the board of directors or between the board and its managers. I attribute this lack of trouble to a policy of complete honesty. When I was offered chances for bribes and commissions, I refused them saying that I would enter no agreement without first discussing it fully with the board of directors. They used to say, 'Oh, Mr. Fast, this is just a little thing.' I said, 'It is not the way we do business.' We always agreed to shake hands at every board meeting to manifest a Christian spirit toward each other.[1]

In these words from the founder, one is able to discern a strong moral and religious tone. Mr. Fast felt a keen sense of responsibility to his fellow members who trusted him with the honored position of head of their mutual organization. The fact that a business concern can operate for almost five decades as a mutual organization without a single misunderstanding of a serious nature is evidence of a generous spirit on the part of both the administration and membership of this organization. The religious note, so evident in this purely commercial organization, may be accounted for by the fact that all of the board members were also church members. Eight of the original nine were members of the Mennonite Church.

Cooperative Creameries

Perhaps, the most frequent activity in which cooperatives find expression in Mennonite communities is among farmers who organize their own creamery associations for the purpose

---
[1] Personal Interview with Herman J. Fast. An examination of the Secretary's minutes confirms this view.

of processing and marketing dairy products. The largest of these cooperative creameries in any Mennonite community is located at Hillsboro, Kansas, where an organization was formed in 1935. The initiative was taken largely by Mennonites in the Hillsboro area. It is operated on the basis of the Rochdale Principles, which means that each member has one vote, that profits are distributed in proportion to the amount of business each person gives to the organization, that there is a fixed interest rate and that only those may belong who produce dairy products.

In 1946, the membership consisted of approximately three thousand farmers, roughly one third of these being Mennonites. This organization has expanded so rapidly that it covers an area from twenty-five to fifty miles beyond the community of Hillsboro. At the present time, this organization is completing a large new half million dollar plant. Butter, cheese, ice cream and all other types of dairy products will be manufactured and distributed as far east as Chicago and New York. In addition, facilities are provided for receiving, grading and storing eggs. The cooperative owns its own trucks for the purpose of collecting milk and eggs, as well as its own large transport units with which to deliver the finished products to distant urban markets.

The question may rightfully be raised as to whether the primary motive in this organization is not more economic than religious. It is a matter of fact that the cooperative now extends far beyond the original Hillsboro community. It enters other territories and competes with other cooperative organizations for milk and eggs.

The reason this organization is included here with the representative types of mutual aid found in Mennonite communities is that it demonstrates an experience common in other Mennonite communities; namely: that an organization started as a small mutual enterprise by a group of church men may so prosper and grow that it tends to lose sight of its original objectives as well as its original spirit. Whether this has happened here, we are not in a position to say, but it should always be remembered that cooperative or mutual organizations are constantly faced with the temptation to surrender the principles of service and brotherhood for dividends, bigness and power just as strictly profit-making commercial agencies are.

At Moundridge, Kansas, about two-thousand farmers own

their own creamery and likewise process dairy products. The farmers in this community also own cooperatively a grain elevator and feed mill, an oil station and a lumber yard. The membership in the Moundridge cooperative organizations is composed largely of members of three branches of Mennonites who live in this area.

In addition to the other cooperative activities listed at Mountain Lake, Minnesota, mention should be made of the cooperative creamery which was organized in 1908 and in 1937 constructed a new $60,000 building. The second story is entirely devoted to a large auditorium which provides a place for farmers to meet and to hold community programs of various sorts. Women in the community, for a time, operated a small library on the second floor in the creamery for the benefit of the local people.

One of the many interesting illustrations of the way in which cooperative creameries develop in Mennonite circles is found in the Amish Mennonite community of Lynnhaven, Virginia. Two brothers, Eli and Elmer Yoder, delivered and bottled milk and cream for retail sale in the city of Norfolk. They started from scratch in 1930 and had a very slow beginning, but by means of hard work and by producing a top quality of milk and rendering conscientious service to their customers, their business grew to where they could no longer supply the demand. The two brothers then took in another Amish neighbor in order to increase the milk supply. Gradually, other Amish neighbors were added until two-hundred gallons of milk a day were sold. Until that time, all milk sold was raw milk. Eventually, it became necessary for all milk dealers to pasteurize their milk and cream as well as to secure a license. The cost of meeting these legal requirements was beyond the ability of the Yoder brothers and their neighbors. Also, quite a number of the other Amish farmers in the community had been separating their milk and selling butter and fresh cream on the Saturday Norfolk markets. The pasteurization orders put a stop to this. The members of the church discussed the problems confronting them and before long, they decided to organize a cooperative as this seemed the only logical way out of their difficulty.

The two brothers sold their business and then were taken into the cooperative as stockholding producers. A charter was drawn up and rules and regulations to operate the business were agreed upon. Among the interesting agreements in the chapter was a decision to have the milk plant closed every Sunday. An extra delivery was to be made on Saturday afternoon instead of one on Sunday. All members had to be producers, and no member could obtain more than twenty shares at $100 a share. At any time more milk was needed, shares were sold and the smallest producer was to be given the first opportunity to buy shares and increase his production. All shareholders were to be members of the Amish Mennonite congregation. Provisions were made in the charter that in case a brother should be excommunicated from the church, he would automatically forfeit his rights in the cooperative, although he was to be reimbursed for his investment in the organization.

The size of this mutual endeavor has increased until it is producing about one thousand, seven-hundred gallons a day. In a financial way, it has been a success and, consequently, added to the financial strength of the members as well as to the congregation and community at large. At the present time, there are approximately thirty members. While there have been many difficulties and obstacles to overcome, the members have maintained a fine cooperative spirit which has enabled the business to remain on a solid foundation and the members feel that this cooperative venture has strengthened the total life of their brotherhood.

Cooperative Oil Stations

In almost all of the Mennonite communities where one finds either cooperative elevators or creameries, one also finds a cooperatively owned and administered oil station service. Since the coming of the tractor and the mechanization of agriculture, farmers are consumers of oil in large quantities. Therefore, it has been found worth while for farmers to pool their resources and organize to help each other. In such thriving Mennonite communities as Souderton and Lancaster, Pennsylvania; Goshen, Indiana; Mountain Lake, Minnesota; Beatrice, Nebraska; Moundridge, Buhler and Goessel, Kansas; Altona, Manitoba and many other communities, Mennonites have taken the initiative in organizing cooperative oil stations or heavily support those that are established.

The large Swiss, Low German and Hutterian Mennonite settlements in and surrounding Freeman, South Dakota support a number of cooperative activities. There are two cooperatively owned gasoline stations, one of which is so unusual that a word of comment is in order. It is known as the College Gasoline Station. It was organized by a number of public spirited citizens in the community during the financial depression of the thirties and then turned over to the Board of Directors of Freeman Junior College to be operated for the benefit of the College. After all expenses are paid, the earnings of the station are turned over to the college. In recent years, this mutual aid technique has been earning approximately $100 per month for the college.

Cooperative Light and Phone Organizations

In almost every state and province where Mennonites are settled, one finds some aspect of mutual aid or cooperative organizations. The variety of such activities is impressive. An illustration of an unusual type of cooperative is found among the Mennonites in Iowa.

As early as 1916, the farmers in the Kalona, Iowa community organized a Cooperative Light and Power Company. It was one of the first mutually owned electric lines in Iowa. In 1914, a group of Amish Mennonites joined their neighbors and organized a mutual telephone company. For many years, the Amish Mennonites of Johnston County, Iowa operated a beef ring during the summer months. This plan called for cooperation on the part of a number of families. Each farmer furnished a beef to be slaughtered by the community butcher every Friday morning. The beef was then divided into as many parts as there were members and distributed to them. In this way, the member families all had fresh meat and yet no family was over burdened with too much at any one time. With the advent of better roads and improved refrigeration, the beef rings were gradually dissolved.

Mutual Aid Burial Plan

The Church of God in Christ, Mennonite congregations located at Copeland, Cimarron, and Montezuma, Kansas have a burial plan based on the principles of mutual aid and Christian simplicity. From among the congregations, a member who is a carpenter is engaged at prevailing rates of pay to serve as a casket maker. He, with the help of his wife, makes the boxes and covers them with the usual plush covering and lines the interior with a white satin. The carpenter usually does this work during the slack seasons of the year when he is not busy with farm work. A half dozen or more caskets of various sizes are made in advance.

In 1945, the cost of a casket was $38. An undertaker was paid $35 for the embalming service, while the grave is dug by relatives or church members as a token of respect and love, thus the total cost of a funeral to the members of this plan is $73. The head of each family in the congregation is assessed two dollars per year to cover the costs. If there are individuals unable to pay their share of these costs, the congregation assumes the expenses for them. Thus every member is assured of a decent funeral and the services for all are practically the same. This low cost service is possible, merely because the people in these congregations quietly work together, plan in advance how they are going to meet unexpected needs and are satisfied with modest funeral services free from pomp and show. This simple plan saves the members about $2,000 a year and more significant than the financial saving is the way members are drawn together in love and Christian fellowship as a result of thus working together.

Spontaneous Mutual Aid

The character of cooperative activity changes from time to time and from place to place as circumstances change. Some forms of mutual activity which were at one time widely practiced have now become extinct, while other forms are now being developed to meet new and emerging conditions. With the coming of a more complex economic order and a more intricate business structure in our society, there is a more noticeable trend in the direction of a more economic base.

Although mutual aid is becoming increasingly more economic and at the same time more systematically organized, the spontaneous and informal aid activities are by no means a thing of the past. This is proved by the frequent demonstrations of it in many communities as reported in such a widely read newspaper as the *Mennonite Weekly Review*. A random selection of cases reported will illustrate the point. In the December 5, 1946 issue, we find the following descriptive paragraph:

Like most Mennonite communities, neighborliness is a habit in the Wellman, Iowa community. But not all communities exhibit this trait on such a large scale as at Wellman. Last week's *Review* carried a story about the 89 persons who gathered at the farm of Mrs. Geneva Hooley and picked 28 acres of corn in one afternoon. On November 19, nineteen neighbors of Mrs. Amy Steckley came to her farm and built a corn crib and on the following Friday fifty-two men came and picked twenty acres of corn which yielded 1,400 bushels. The same Friday, a group of seventy-eight persons came together at the Noah Mast home and picked 1,800 bushels of corn in the afternoon. Mr. Mast has been unable to do work because of illness.

In the July 20, 1941 issue of the *Review*, the following item is reported:

Realizing that their neighbor, C. F. Funk, one and one-half miles east of the Alexanderwohl Church, was in need of help, nineteen farmers with tractors and plows moved in on his farm last Saturday and plowed 100 acres of wheatland in six hours. Mr. Funk is recovering from serious injuries suffered while cutting wheat with a binder on June 18 when his clothing caught in the power take-off.

In the January 19, 1939 issue of the *Belleville, Pennsylvania Times*, the following item is reported about an Amish group in Pennsylvania. Among the Amish, spontaneous mutual aid is often the custom rather than the exception:

To those who know and understand the Amish people, it is no surprise that a new barn stands today on the John D. Byler farm near Wilmington, Pennsylvania, where only several days ago was nothing but a foundation and several piles of lumber . . . Last Thursday morning, ninety Amish farmers from all parts of this territory turned their buggies into the drive of the Byler farm. They placed timber for the framework of the barn in strategic spots about the foundation of the old barn which was destroyed by fire last fall. Nobody loafed, everyone knew what to do. In just one hour after the timber began to go up, the framework was in place—which must be some sort of an unrecorded record . . . By noon the siding was ready to be put on.

In the meantime, the Amish women folk were preparing dinner—a working-man's dinner . . . Today the barn, which is not a small one, the dimensions being 45 feet by

57 feet with a shed 26 feet by 30 feet is nearly complete. It will be completed next week, Mr. Byler said. Which shows how the Amish folks do things . . . 'It's another way in which we people help each other,' said Mr. Byler.

At Inman, Kansas, mutual aid serves as the device by which one church raises money to support its minister. In the July 31, 1940 issue of the *Review*, the following item is reported:

Forty acres of wheat rented from Paul D. Kaufman, and farmed by members of the Inman Mennonite Church is found to be a substantial help in paying the pastor's salary. The tract of wheat land was plowed and seeded last fall, as well as harvested this summer, as a church enterprise.

These few representative illustrations are testimony to the fact that the spirit of love for one's neighbor, the desire to be mutually helpful and the sense of concern for the welfare of others is not mere theory or an abstract ideal. It is an evidence that love is alive and active within numerous congregational fellowships. What has been done and is constantly being done in the few communities mentioned might well serve to stimulate other Christian groups to cultivate this same spirit and practice.

SUGGESTIONS:

1. Make a list of the mutual aid practices in your community. Distinguish between mutual aid that is expressed through an organization and that which is a result of neighborliness.

2. Write to the author of this pamphlet describing organizations and acts of mutual aid that illustrate Christian brotherhood.

QUESTIONS:

1. How does mutual aid in the United States today differ from Mennonite mutual aid in the past?

2. Is mutual aid practiced more by older settlers or by recent immigrants?

3. What changes are taking place in the types of mutual aid practiced in the United States?

4. Are cooperatives supplementing or replacing mutual aid organizations?

5. What lessons can cooperative organizations and mutual aid societies learn from each other?

VII

Mennonites Practice Mutual Aid Today—Continued

"By their fruits ye shall know them." Matt. 6:50.

Canada

It is well to give attention to mutual aid and cooperative developments among Mennonites in Canada and the three Latin American countries where Mennonites have found refuge from European terror and tyranny in this generation. In Canada especially, some Mennonite communities have developed more comprehensive mutual aid and cooperative activities than have Mennonites anywhere else in the world. This is partially due to the fact that many Canadian Mennonites are settled in compact communities and are homogeneous in character. It is also due, in part, to the fact that some of the Mennonite settlements were composed of refugee immigrants from Russia who were often compelled to practice mutual aid in order to survive. A third factor accounting for the development of cooperative interest among the Canadian Mennonites is the general influence of the American Cooperative Movement which has grown rapidly in power and economic significance in recent decades.

Southern Manitoba

The Southern Manitoba Mennonites who settled in what is known as the West Reserve, about 75 miles southwest of the city of Winnipeg, in the 1870's have developed an amazing amount of cooperative interest and activity within the past fifteen years. It is as if a latent power long held in subjection had finally broken through its confinement walls and was suddenly pervading its entire surrounding territory. For a few of the Mennonite communities it has meant a virtual economic and social rebirth.

The little town of Altona with a population of approximately one thousand inhabitants, of which ninety-eight percent are Mennonites, demonstrates the effect of the sudden discovery of the cooperative philosophy and technique. The initial stimulus for the development of cooperatives came out of the economic crisis caused by the depression years of the thirties. A number of farmers in the community first organized the Rhineland Agricultural Society and out of the study and discussions of this group came the beginnings of a number of cooperative organizations. Several mutual aid societies existed a long time before the cooperatives were organized but these have been incorporated and modified recently to meet the demands of the times.

A Mennonite Burial Society which had been organized in 1910 was reorganized in 1940. The Red River Mutual Fire Insurance Company which had been operating for many years as an unchartered aid society was chartered in 1941. A Consumers Cooperative Oil and Gas Service station was organized in 1931 with approximately 300 members. A general store known as the Altona Cooperative Service, Limited, was organized in 1937 by ten men who subscribed $45.00 in capital and borrowed $600.00 to buy stock. This organization in 1946 was owned by over 800 heads of families in the community and had assets valued at over $92,000.00. The annual sales in this cooperative store have amounted to over a quarter million dollars. It is one of the largest and best equipped rural general stores to be found anywhere in Canada.

A credit union was organized in 1939 with 316 members. A cooperative hatchery was organized a year later. In 1943, a group of local farmers who had become accustomed to depending on themselves for the solution of their problems, decided to organize a farmers cooperative machine shop. This was to meet the problems they faced due to inability to buy new parts or to get prompt repair service due to severe labor shortages and the closing of a number of repair shops. The cooperative machine shop provided employment for seven men, and during the first year of operation cash income from sales and service amounted to over $24,000.

Cooperative Vegetable Oils, Limited, is the most recent of the cooperative organizations in the Altona community. It is a plant built for the purpose of extracting oil from sunflower seeds, soy beans and other oil producing vegetables. It is owned by approximately 2000 farmers and was erected at a cost of $125,000. The plant was completed and dedicated in April of 1946. This enterprise alone promises to make a tremendous contribution to the economic development of the community by shifting the economic base from a single crop, which previously was wheat, to a variety of oil producing crops for which there now is a ready market. The fact that these ventures have been mutual enterprises rather than individually owned enterprises means that increased economic prosperity is distributed into the hands of many rather than kept in the pockets of a few. The community of Altona has set an example in rural community economic revival to which all of Manitoba has been paying attention and to which Mennonites far and wide might profitably go to learn.

Altona is not alone in its development in mutual aid activity among the Mennonite communities in southern Manitoba. There are twenty-six cooperative organizations in this area, all of them in Mennonite communities. These twenty-six organizations have formed what is called the Federation of Southern Manitoba Cooperatives. At the annual meeting of this Federation held in July, 1946, it was reported that there were three oil stations, seven stores, six producers cooperatives, and nine credit unions, which had done almost one and a half million dollars worth of business during 1945. Newly organized cooperatives that were introduced at the 1946 meeting were a bakery, a cannery, three egg grading stations, and the previously mentioned Vegetable Oils Plant. The location of other cooperative activities in this area are at Gretna, Winkler, Rhineland, Morris, and Plum Coulee. Mennonites in these communities are discovering that through mutual efforts they are able to solve their economic problems without government aid and in keeping with Christian ethical business methods.

British Columbia

Another illustration of a contemporary effort among the Mennonites in Canada is that of the recent settlements in British Columbia. Coming to the Frazer Valley of British Columbia as penniless refugees from Russia in 1928, these people at first worked as day laborers for as little as 15 cents an hour in the hop vineyards. After experimenting with various fruit and vegetable crops, they found that berries yielded the best results. Today raspberry and strawberry patches and fruit orchards can be found on almost all of the more than 700 Mennonite homes in the Frazer Valley area. In 1937 the

Mennonites organized the Yarrow Growers Cooperative Union and one year later began to process berries for shipment to eastern markets. Some berries are sold fresh but most of them are chemically treated and packed in 400 pound barrels and sold to distant markets.

In 1946 Yarrow alone is reported to have had 350 acres of berries. The community has also established a cooperative store and more recently a jam factory. Recently all of the cooperative organizations in the Frazer Valley settlements have formed one central organization. This includes the cooperative activities formerly operated separately at Sardis and Abbotsford. The membership in the cooperative in 1945 was 450 doing almost a million dollars worth of business. In addition to the large cooperative enterprise in the Yarrow community are the following privately owned ventures: a produce station, a cold storage locker system, a berry box factory, a grain elevator, two lumber yards, and a general store. Here, too, the power of mutual aid has demonstrated its worth; without united efforts these refugee settlers could not have successfully pioneered and succeeded as they have today.

Alberta

Another illustration of mutual aid among the Mennonites in Canada is found in Coaldale, Alberta, where a Mennonite Health Society has been organized. This society reflects the community solidarity of the Mennonite settlement. It is a systematic plan whereby medical attention is provided for the members of the community at rock bottom rates. The society in 1943 had a membership of 300. The cost of medical services in 1943 was $9.25 per family per year, or $6.00 per single person and $4.50 for widows. Undoubtedly in recent years the rates have increased somewhat along with the general rise in the price level.

The origin of this health plan goes back to Russia where these people had their own medical doctors and hospitals. When they came to Coaldale they found hospital and medical expenses were prohibitive. The impoverished settlers were shocked to discover that a tonsillectomy cost $60.00 and a doctor's death certificate from $10.00 to $15.00. The writer was told of numerous instances where people already in financial difficulties were completely submerged with debt when they encountered medical expenses. As a result of this situation the Coaldale Mennonites studied the possibility of group medical protection.

At Lethbridge, a city ten miles distant, their group efforts were discouraged by hospital authorities. Arrangements were finally made with an individual doctor in the city on the basis of $12.00 per family on condition that the families would call at his office. This did not prove satisfactory and in a few years the community called its own Mennonite doctor from Saskatchewan who still serves as resident physician. There was a set fee of $35.00 for major operations and $10.00 for all minor operations, and $15.00 for confinement cases in the hospital. Home calls at night were $2.00 plus 35c mileage charge one way. The day mileage charge was 25c one way. This was in contrast to the standard charge of $1.00 per mile which the Lethbridge doctors had been charging the Coaldale residents.

When one considers the number of preventive cases and others where individuals were improved through medical attention in proper time the saving in the course of a year is tremendous. The doctor's report for 1942 indicated that there were 1,936 office calls, 106 home calls, 28 major operations, 71 minor operations, 390 tooth extractions, 33 fractures and dislocations, 57 confinement cases, and 4 deaths. The spiritual satisfactions and sense of security that come from having an adequate health program available locally and at a reasonable cost cannot be measured financially. The cooperative plan demonstrated in Coaldale, Alberta, is practical for hundreds of other Mennonite communities in the United States and Canada.

Separate from the Health Society but a community enterprise is the local thirteen bed hospital. A country school building was moved to town and later an addition built on. Today it provides splendid community service for the sick. Over three hundred patients are treated annually and three nurses are engaged. In addition to the hospital and health plan, Coaldale also has a thriving cooperative creamery which was organized by the Mennonites.

Ontario

The Mennonite immigrants who came to Canada in the twenties for the most part settled in the Prairie Provinces. In recent years there have been heavy migrations west to British Columbia and east to Ontario. The communities of Vineland and Virgil in Ontario lie along the shores of the western end of Lake Ontario. The Mennonite settlers who came here had very little, if any, money, but they had ingenuity and perseverance and a willingness to help each other. Large farms were purchased and divided, into five, ten, and fifteen acre tracts. These were originally bought by one or two of the more enterprising and adventuresome Mennonite refugees. The small plots were bought on a ten percent down payment basis. The purchasers were very eager to own their own homes and were willing to start on a low plane of living. The dwelling quarters at first were often one or two-room frame shelters that later were used as chicken houses. Fruit trees and vegetables were immediately planted and while waiting for these to produce, husbands and wives and often entire families worked as day laborers in surrounding communities. The combined earnings provided income to purchase food and to meet financial obligations incurred in the purchase of land.

Mennonites organized the Niagara Fruit Cooperative to serve as a marketing agency for the produce of the Mennonite fruit and vegetable farms in the area. Two branch associations of the Cooperative have been established—one three miles from Virgil and the other in St. Catharines. In addition to the cooperative mentioned, one of the enterprising refugees established a large cannery at Virgil. This enterprise provides employment for about 200 women and 50 men. It also provides a way of preserving highly perishable fruit and vegetables and thus prevents large annual losses due to spoilage or inability to sell advantageously on the fresh fruit market.

Mexico

An illustration of mutual aid among contemporary Mennonites is found in Mexico. The 12,000 Mennonites in Mexico are located for the most part in two large settlements in the States of Chihuahua and Durango. All but about one hundred of these are members of the Sommerfelder or the Old Colony Mennonites, who came from Canada in the twenties. The Mennonites in Mexico are settled in large compact colonies in villages of fifty to three hundred individuals per village. The church is the central organization around which all of life revolves. Each colony has a Waisenamt. This organization operates perhaps more nearly like that of the older Waisenamts in Russia than any other Mennonite activity. It is the chief mutual aid agency in the colony.

At each church in the colony there is a small granary where members contribute grain such as oats, beans, corn, or wheat; also cash contributions are received. The money and the grain is in charge of the deacons who buy flour and other commodities that are needed by some of the poor in the colony. The grain is often collected by one of the villagers who goes from home to home and village to village with a wagon and collects from each farmer several bushels at a time. This grain is sometimes given to the poor for seed as well as for feed. Those who receive this help may pay it back to the common granary if in later years they are able.

Land Settlement

The Mennonites in Mexico, as in other parts of the world, constantly face the problem of securing new land for their ever-growing population. The method by which they meet this problem, however, is unique among contemporary Mennonites and for this reason will be described here. It is a very direct carry over from the land settlement practices among the Mennonites in Russia. This method, however, differs from any method used in America today. The striking difference is the systematic way in which land is acquired and developed. When there is a growing consciousness in the colony that new land is needed, the Oberschulz (colony leader) and his assistants take the initiative in scouting for new land, as well as in discovering who in the colony wants the land.

The procedure is as follows: A list of the names of people wanting new land is drawn up and each man states the amount of land desired and the amount of money available for purchase of the land. If he does not have sufficient funds of his own he is urged to borrow the money from a friend or relative. Money not available for purchase from those who want the land is generally supplied by the men with means in the colony on a loan basis. The creditors receive three or four per cent interest and the borrowers pay six per cent; the difference being used to defray administrative costs. The total acreage purchased by the colony is always larger than the immediate demand so that there is room for expansion.

The interested group of settlers meet with the Oberschulz to draw up a plan of division for the new settlement. The whole new area is plotted into several villages and each village divided into separate farm homesteads. Each plot or separate farm is given a number. When the total plan is worked out, the interested parties draw lots for the number of the farm they are to buy. After the selection, if two individuals wish to exchange their plots, they may do so, but they cannot refuse their farm outright in favor of another drawing. Each farm is evaluated in advance according to the quality of the land and its location. Hence the several farms vary in price.

Each new village then organizes by electing its own schulz (village leader) as well as choosing other public officials and a name for the village. The name is usually a favorite one found among the familiar ones of Mennonite villages in Canada or Russia. In 1946 the Old Colony purchased a tract of land consisting of 72,000 acres at a cost of 4,872,000 pesos or Mexican dollars. In United States dollars this amounts to $374,500. This systematic method of solving such a basic problem suggests that the Mennonite policy of land settlement in Mexico might be studied and used by Christian groups in many parts of the world. Individual men in need could not have undertaken this huge project, but by means of the strong helping the weak, of brother helping brother, and by pooling resources and working together, great things can be done.

Paraguay

The Mennonites in Paraguay came from Canada and from Russia. Those from Russia spent several years in Germany as refugees. After the doors of Paraguay had been opened for the refugee Mennonites, an MCC representative went to Germany to organize the immigrant Mennonites before leaving for Paraguay. Once in Paraguay the Mennonites adopted a plan of cooperative organization to carry on economic activities. All of the business with the outside world such as buying and selling of economic produce, contact with political officials of Paraguay, relations with the Mennonite Central Committee, and the like are carried on through the colony's central cooperative organization. Individual private businesses are permitted within the colony but any commodities produced for export must pass through the agency of the central cooperative.

Cooperative Enterprise

The cooperative society, which in this case is synonymous with the entire community, also operates a number of the colony industries such as a cotton gin, peanut-oil factory, saw mill, creamery, cheese factory, and retail stores. The cooperative serves as a community bank; not as an organized bank in the recognized sense, but as a credit agency and a depository and a buying and selling agency. Other community mutual aid facilities are a fire protection system, a mutual fire insurance society, a hospital, and a mutual benefit society connected with the hospital. Each member of the community pays a certain amount per month and receives all medical protection and care.

An illustration of the necessity of mutual aid or cooperation is the matter of getting credit. Organized as a community cooperative and serving as an agent for the individuals in the community, the cooperative is able to get credit in foreign countries whereas individuals cannot. During a drought in 1935-36 the cooperative organization was able to secure loans from sources outside the colony and thus tide over many of the families that were hardest hit. These hardpressed individuals would never have been able to secure such loans on their own. The cooperative organization was also able to import goods into the community for a period of ten years free of charge whereas individuals did not have the same privilege. Furthermore, mutual efforts were necessary in order to start new industries. No single individual or family had sufficient capital to undertake such an enterprise but when all hands joined together, it was possible to accomplish the desires of the group.

Achievements

Anyone familiar with the achievements of the Mennonites in Paraguay must marvel at their envious record. In the Chaco, referred to by the Paraguayans as the "Green Hell" because they believed it to be a vast jungle area uninhabitable by man, the Mennonites settled. In this barren spot, in the most central part of Latin America, the Mennonites carved out homes, established villages, developed the soil, and planted a Christian society of almost 5000 souls. They were able to accomplish this only because of cooperation with God and fellowman. Not the least of this cooperation was the aid of the Mennonites in North America.

A recent comment on the importance of cooperation among the Mennonites in Paraguay by Orie O. Miller, Executive Secretary of the Mennonite Central Committee is of interest here. He said: "I knew nothing about cooperatives in 1931, but I with their leaders went out under a shade tree one afternoon and we organized a cooperative known as the Fernheim Cooperative. That was the name under which it was incorporated in Paraguay; that was the instrument through which the brethren there decided to take care of themselves during the pioneer days. And as I look back over the past fifteen years there, I have a deep conviction that if they had not put into it through the years the Christianity of which they were capable, they couldn't have come through. And it is a sample, it seems to me, of something of the kind that we as a people do well to take into account."[1]

The power and effectiveness of mutual aid as a survival technique for a religious refugee group such as the Mennonites is clearly demonstrated in the case of this Paraguayan settlement. Everyone who had any official connection with the transplanting of this group of over two thousand individuals admits that it was only the practice of mutual aid that made existence possible. It was mutual aid among the refugee brethren as well as mutual aid between the refugees and their brethren in the rest of the world that made possible the escape from Russia; it was mutual aid that secured for them a temporary shelter in Germany; it was mutual aid that provided transportation to Paraguay; it was mutual aid that advanced them credit for the purchase of land, stock, food, and equipment in their new wilderness home and it is the continuing practice of mutual aid at the present time that enables the colony to exist and grow.

Brazil

The Mennonite settlers in Brazil like those in Paraguay were stationed for a number of years in Germany following their flight from Russia. Unlike the Mennonites in Paraguay, however, the Mennonite Central Committee did not assist the Mennonites coming to Brazil. Those settling in Brazil were aided chiefly by the Dutch Mennonites and by the German Government. The latter had guaranteed the Mennonite colonists support for one year from the time of arrival. Soon after landing

[1] Orie O. Miller, "The Industrial Relations Outlook for the Future," *The Gospel Herald*, May 14, 1946. p. 148.

in Brazil, the agent of the German Government took the initiative in establishing a colony economic organization known as the Witmarsum Cooperative Agricultural Society. Every refugee family was to be a member of this cooperative. The Dutch Mennonites advanced the necessary funds to build two flour mills, two saw mills, and several stores. In addition they furnished money for schools, for medical aid and one cow for each family.

The colonists faced the usual list of pioneer difficulties. One especially difficult problem in Brazil was that of marketing aipim, a root crop with a very high starch content. The distance of forty miles to the nearest railway station meant high cost to transport this crop. In fact the cost of transportation about equalled the sale value of the product. It was evident that if the starch could be refined locally and the finished product shipped, it would be a great saving to the colonists. This, however, required a considerable amount of capital which the refugees did not have. Here again Christian mutual aid demonstrated its merit. The Dutch Mennonites learned of this need and advanced the money for the construction of a starch factory. This meant a great deal for the economic welfare of the Brazilian Mennonites at Witmarsum.

A Testimony to Mutual Aid

A testimony to the sustaining power of mutual aid among the Mennonites in Brazil is given by Peter Klassen, one of the colony leaders. He said: "Only one who has had the opportunity to observe how the unorganized German colonists in this country have had to struggle in desperation and often practically sell themselves to the private merchants in the colonies in order to get credit, can appreciate what a blessing the cooperative has been for our colony, and still is. In the other settlements many have had to give up. We thank God and our brethren who have made it possible to establish our cooperative. And then in May, 1932, a small almost unnoticeable creamery was established in Witmarsum. If this last enterprise had not been established, it is doubtful whether we would have been able to conduct our cooperative on an even partially sound basis. Without it we would probably have dragged ourselves along on a miserably low scale of economic attainment."[1]

---

1 Peter Klassen, "Mennonites In Brazil," *M.Q.R.* XI (April, 1937) p. 110.

MENNONITES PRACTICE MUTUAL AID TODAY   61

The conclusion is inescapable that Mennonites are still practicing mutual aid. The variety of organizations and types of cooperative expression is much larger than in former days. There is also a noticeable trend in the direction of more systematic organizations on a cooperative basis among Mennonites today than formerly. In addition to the mutual aid insurance societies and burial associations founded years ago, Mennonites today are practicing mutual aid in such businesses as creameries, grain elevators, oil stations, and stores. The motivation seems to be twofold: one religious, growing out of the earlier mutual aid insurance societies and the other economic, growing out of needs of the times as well as the general stimulus from the present growing cooperative movement. Cooperative organizations may have religious motivation but in some Mennonite and in many non-Mennonite cooperative organizations the religious motive is sadly beclouded, if not absent entirely. It is to be hoped that with a revival of interest in mutual aid within the Mennonite Church and a rediscovery of the Christian philosophy underlying it, present day mutual aid will become spiritually enriched instead of materialistic and selfish. Strengthening the Christian community, love of the brotherhood, and service, should be the primary goals of all mutual aid activities whether organized or unorganized, economic or benevolent in character.

SUGGESTIONS:

1. Make a list of services that could be advantageously performed by means of mutual aid in your community?

2. Send a description of some mutual aid activitiy in your community to the author of this pamphlet.

QUESTIONS:

1. Are mutual aid activities more common among the older settlers in Canada or among the recent immigrants?

2. What differences do you note between the mutual aid practiced in Canada and that practiced in Mexico, Paraguay and Brazil?

3. How can the religious motive be retained and strengthened in co-operative organizations?

4. What are you doing to develop the spirit and practice of Christian mutual aid in your community?

5. Can the land settlement method of the Mennonites in Mexico be adapted for use in the United States or Canada?

VIII

Present Day Needs For Mutual Aid

"Bear ye one another's burdens and so fulfill the law of Christ." Gal. 6:2.

The need for bearing one another's burdens in a material and a spiritual sense is as great today as it ever was. Mutual aid as a Christian practice is never out of date. The spirit of love and brotherhood needs to saturate men so thoroughly that it will become the basic motivation for every act of their lives. Many of the apostolic Christians and many of our Mennonite forefathers seem to have been so saturated. They were more continually God-conscious than most Christians in our time seem to be. Brotherhood was not merely a name which one occasionally used as another way of referring to the church. Brotherhood was their business. As members of the reborn in Christ they felt constrained always to love and serve the brotherhood. This fact is reflected in their attitude toward property, toward charging or receiving interest and in their willingness to share house and home and all material goods with those who were in need.

It is the purpose of this pamphlet to reawaken in the minds of its readers this ardor for brotherhood; this desire for a thorough-going practice of Christianity by those who profess it as a faith and a way of life. It is hoped that the rediscovery of a sense of genuine brotherhood will again restore the practice of Christian mutual aid to its rightful place in the Church.

In this chapter, we shall suggest three areas in which mutual aid should be more fully and intensively developed. The purpose of these few suggestions may stimulate the imagination of our people to become an effective leaven in the total life of the Church. Christian mutual aid should again become the distinguishing characteristic of the way true disciples perform their common tasks and exercise their stewardship over their God-given talents and possessions.

Christian Channels For Investing Money

Thus far no one has made a study of the way Mennonites invest their money. Such a study would be in order and should prove interesting and highly profitable. One thing is certain, however, and that is that many Mennonites have substantial amounts of money to invest. The Mennonite custom of working hard, saving much and spending little is bound to produce financial surpluses. After he has paid for his home, cleared his debts, and has his daily needs provided for how should a Mennonite invest his money? Many devout brothers are sincerely asking this question. Is there a place within the brotherhood where one may confidently invest his surplus funds in such a way as to be mutually beneficial to borrower and lender alike?

To date Mennonites have paid too little attention to this question and hence have had no satisfactory answer. As a result Mennonites have invested their savings in a wide variety of secular enterprises over which they had no control and by means of which they sometimes aided businesses engaged in activities which were contrary to Mennonite religious principles. Stocks and bonds bought from brokers and investment bankers may pay handsome dividends, be highly recommended as gilt edge securities, and seem innocent enough on paper. Nevertheless, from the point of view of Mennonite ethical principles it would seem glaringly inconsistent to own shares in such corporations as the United States Steel, the Standard Oil of New Jersey, the Anaconda Copper, General Motors, General Electric and a thousand others who engage wholeheartedly in manufacturing war products and prosecuting a war. Even public utilities, in which Mennonites frequently invest, may engage in irregular and corrupt practices but which Mennonites as shareholders have little power to influence or correct. Thus the practice of investing funds in modern corporation securities should at least be made the subject of careful examination by the sincere Christian who claims to have a tender conscience on such matters as materialism, worldliness, exploitation, and participation in war.

In a religious body such as the Mennonite Church which exalts simplicity as a virtue it is also proper to raise a question about the consistency of investing surplus money in land to the point of excluding others who need it for the basic purpose of making a living. There are practices on the part of individuals in many Mennonite communities of accumulating land by buying farm after farm merely for the sake of investment, not because they need them to make a living for themselves, their sons or sons-in-law, nor even to make efficient sized farm units. This tendency toward land monopoly is a very old evil. Already in the eighth century before Christ, Isaiah condemns the practice. "Woe unto them that join house to house, that lay field to field, till there be no place, that they may be placed alone in the midst of the earth." (Isaiah 5:8).

The reasons why these monopolistic practices are evil are: first, it is a form of selfishness, a manifestation of lust for economic power and this world's goods. Furthermore, it denies other brethren in the community with less means, and perhaps greater need of the land, the opportunity to secure the land. Such men may have sons who want to establish themselves locally and become permanent members of the Mennonite community but cannot because there is no land available. It is wrong also because since one man cannot farm all the land he acquires he must hire other men to work for him as hired men or as tenants, but in both cases he keeps brethren who desire ownership of a farm in the landless and propertyless class. The land monopolist denies others the chance to become owners. Such unwholesome practices in any community cause envy, strife, jealousy, and ill feelings. They create dissension and unchristian attitudes within the brotherhood. Thus selfish use of money among Mennonites is a threat to Christian harmony and unity.

Another unfortunate fact so far as Mennonite investments are concerned is the tremendous financial losses that have resulted from investing money in various unsound and unscrupulous real estate promoters schemes. It is a strange and unexplainable fact that some of the most careful and conservative spenders of money among the brethren have been victimized by some of the wildest and most fantastic investment proposals. Clever promoters of money-making schemes have in times past found sober Mennonites their most gullible customers.

It is sufficient to say that the unsound investments have resulted not only in heavy financial losses, but in tremendous spiritual losses as well. Church members who moved away from the home community to become a part of an unsuccessful land settlement venture frequently drifted into non-Mennonite communities, joined other churches, or remained unchurched in the area after all but a few of the Mennonite settlers had moved out. Those who returned to their home churches and communities were generally poorer than when they left and thus had to start over again. Those who were of middle age by this time were frequently too discouraged and tired to put forth much effort toward their personal rehabilitation, thus they became a problem to themselves and to their brotherhood. The history of bad financial investments by Mennonites is a sad story.

There are those among the Mennonites with money to invest, who, like the man with the one talent in the parable told by Jesus, are so cautious of losing what they have that they allow it to lie idle rather than risk it by helping a brother. This policy affords a certain amount of personal safety and a sense of security but it automically prevents the money from being used to help promote some worthy cause or some deserving brother.

In the foregoing illustrations of unwise investment of funds, the chief criticism is that primary consideration was not given to the greatest good for the greatest number. The primary consideration in every case was individual benefit and individual enrichment. Certainly the devout Christian will want to act unselfishly. He will want to give careful thought to the way his investments, as well as his conduct, affect others. He will make every effort to see that he does not make personal gain at the expense of his fellowmen. Sincere Christians are concerned that their investments are mutually beneficial. They should benefit the other person or the public as well as the investor.

A primary present day need for mutual aid among Mennonites then is to develop Christian investment opportunities for individuals with money to invest. Such opportunities would enable the more well-to-do Mennonites to use their money to the benefit of others, especially "within the household of faith." It would not be expected that such funds would be given as charity but rather that they would become available for use on a loan basis. Interest for the use of the money could be charged or not according to the conscience of the investor. It should be remembered, however, that there is nothing sacred or holy about the charging of interest. For many centuries Christians considered it a sin to do so and

Mennonites, almost longer than any other Protestants, forbade it as an unscriptural practice. It is, therefore, both legally permissible and perfectly honorable for one Christian brother to make a loan to another without charging interest. If interest is to be charged it should certainly not be usurious.

It is gratifying to note that a small beginning has been made in the direction of providing an investment channel for Mennonites such as we are discussing by at least two Mennonite groups. The (Old) Mennonites in 1944 organized an agency known as Mennonite Mutual Aid Incorporated. This is not an official church organization, although it has conference approval. The General Conference of Mennonites organized The Board of Mutual Aid in 1945 as an official phase of its Conference program. One of the functions of these newly created agencies is to provide places for men with a desire to render Christian service to invest their money. Other Mennonite groups are seeing the need for similar action and are taking steps to provide similar opportunities although in a more informal way.

Mennonite groups are doing their members a genuine service by organizing such investment opportunities. There are many within the brotherhood who have sincerely been seeking such a service. A few statements from letters to the writer are indications of this fact. "Some time ago I sold a house . . . and have $1000 which I would like to loan without interest to some cause that would do good somewhere. Could it be used?" A widowed sister writes: "I have been praying about this and debating where I could do the most good with about $500." A brother says: "Find enclosed a check for $3000 to loan to needy boys without interest to me for not more than five years." Individual Mennonites are interested in developing forms of Christian mutual aid. The individual congregations and conference groups must nurture and guide those interests into fruitful avenues.

Giving Youth a Financial Start

The second urgent need for the development of mutual aid in our day is a systematic and orderly plan of providing financial assistance to young people in getting a vocational start in life. The group needing such help constitutes a minority but it is an important minority. It is composed of individuals who have qualities of leadership and capacities to develop into useful Christian citizens but whose hopes are often shattered and capacities undeveloped because of lack of opportunity. There are those who have ability to farm but never get a chance; there are others with ability to manage business enterprises who never do because they have no chance to begin; there are those with alert minds and love of learning who never go on to school because of a lack of funds.

Such needy young people happen to be born into families where parents are unable to give their children the kind of help they need. If the necessary resources cannot be found within the circle of relatives the logical place for young people to look for help is within the brotherhood of which they are members. At present some find help in the brotherhood but many do not. There is need for the establishment of a systematic plan of providing aid, a plan that is recognized by the whole brotherhood so that those with money and those in need of money will understand and use the plan.

Common financial needs of young people are: sufficient funds to marry and establish a home, funds to buy livestock and equipment to start farming, funds to buy or rent a farm, funds to establish a privately owned business, funds to secure an education. There are many Mennonite communities which need Christian medical doctors and there are many Christian young men who would like to become doctors, but communities fail to get medical men and the young men fail to become doctors because the young men lack the finances to go through medical school and communities lack plans for helping their would-be doctors attain their goals.

With the increasing mechanization of farming comes also the increased cost of getting started on the farm. It is no longer practical for a young farmer to start with a pair of horses, a wagon and a plow. Today he needs a tractor, a disc, grain drill, mower, binder and a car. Instead of a $200 minimum today it is a $2,000 minimum even with this figure he must depend on a father, brother, or neighbor to use a considerable number of essential tools and implements. But even this minimum is not easily and quickly saved. When earnings are high so is the cost of living; when prices are low so is the rate of earning.

If the Mennonite Church values its youth, it will make plans to provide mutual help for them. If it makes no such plans the loss of youth will be greater than it has been in the past. It will mean that an increasing number of farm boys will be driven to a life-time of service as hired men or tenant farmers, or it will mean that they leave the farm and take their places among the ranks of laboring men in industry. If no help is provided for those wanting to establish themselves in a commercial or a manufacturing business of their own, they will also join the millions of wage earners in modern business and industry and thus join the army of insecure propertyless laborers whose restlessness today is the cause of much industrial conflict.

The modern laborer is a landless, propertyless and often helpless individual. He has no share in the ownership of the plant or business where he works. He owns none of the tools or the machines with which he works. If he loses his job he loses his means of earning bread and butter. The uncertainty of his job and the unsteadiness of his work create in him a gnawing sense of insecurity. To overcome his feeling of helplessness and sense of insecurity he joins a labor union. The union guarantees him a measure of protection by helping him fight for his job and steady employment and it provides for him a sense of solidarity and strength that he needs to compensate for his feeling of insecurity.

There is nothing morally wrong with being a laboring man either on the farm or in industry but most industrious young people have aspirations of becoming owners. With ownership come certain spiritual satisfactions that are not found in the rank of the wage earner. Ownership affords certain creative opportunities in the field of Christian stewardship and it affords certain measures of individual freedom not open to the man who works for another as a laborer.

The value of ownership as a desirable personal goal is reflected in a poll of vocational preferences of CPS men. Of all the men in CPS camps as of March 1, 1944, 60% wanted to enter farming; 9% wanted to establish themselves in business; 5% wanted to become teachers; 6% wanted to enter some phase of full-time religious work; 9% wanted to follow one of the skilled trades, while only 2% expressed a preference for office work, and 3% indicated an interest in factory work.

Since most of the men have been discharged from CPS they have had a chance to pursue these vocational choices. All indications are that there is little departure from the prefer-

PRESENT DAY NEEDS FOR MUTUAL AID

ences expressed while in camp. The largest number of requests for aid from CPS men have been for financial loans to help them start farming. Requests for loans for purchasing of a tractor or a grain drill, loans for a few head of livestock, loans for household equipment such as kitchen ranges, heating stoves, refrigerators and furniture, loans for a car or truck, loans for a portion of the payment of a house or a farm have been frequent. Others have requested aid from church groups for funds to establish themselves in business or to complete their programs of education if they wished to prepare for such fields as teaching, medicine, law, engineering and accounting.

If Mennonite groups are prepared to provide the kind of financial assistance needed by their young people it will mean that Mennonite youth may be expected to look to their church rather than to the government for aid. If young people look to the church for aid the church is in a position to give them guidance and spiritual counsel as well. If the church turns its needy youth to secular channels for economic aid it may well expect youth to turn to such channels for the solutions to other problems as well.

In addition to the need for a program of mutual aid for individuals in local communities and congregations there is also the need for providing financial assistance to individuals and groups leaving the home communities and establishing new settlements. In such settlements it is unusual for any single colonist to have sufficient capital to establish community economic enterprises. The lack of such enterprises handicap the entire settlement. If the handicaps are too great and economic reverses set in, settlers become discouraged and one after another leaves. In so doing the discouraged are likely to lose the original investment plus incurring the costs of migrating again and of becoming established a second time.

Mennonites have been concerned about helping their brethren become established after they fled from one land to another. This is praiseworthy but they should be no less concerned about helping those within their own land who seek to establish themselves in new settlements. It is entirely possible that the Section for Mennonite Aid under the Mennonite Central Committee will become an agency for this purpose. Various Mennonite groups may either establish their own systems of providing colonization and resettlement aid or they may work cooperatively with each other through the Mennonite Aid Section.

Providing Information and Counsel

The two previous topics of this chapter dealt with aspects of finances; one discussed the proper use of surplus funds and the other suggested the kind of purposes for which such funds were needed. The third need for mutual aid does not deal with money but rather with the general subject of information and counsel.

One of the discoveries made in CPS was that large numbers of young men were quite undecided about basic issues in life. Many were uncertain what they should do with their lives; what kind of work they should take up; what their personalities were best fitted for; where there was need for the kind of services and skills they felt able to contribute; where they should locate geographically; whether they should buy or rent a farm; whether they should move to a new community or remain in the old one. These and dozens of similar questions were on the minds of Mennonite young men in Civilian Public Service. It is probable that such questions are on the minds of the youth of every generation. Such young people are looking to someone for answers; they are seeking guidance, information and help. Who is to give them this help? Where are they to go for answers? To parents, to pastors, to friends, yes, but unless parents, pastors and friends have made a special effort to inform themselves, they may not be prepared to provide complete and satisfactory answers. Not all well-meaning fathers are able to give sound vocational advice, and not all pastors are able to devote the time they would like to this phase of their work.

The suggestion here is that Mennonite congregations might well consider the electing of mutual aid committees to assist in the carrying out of this mutual aid function. Such committees would not be all-wise but if chosen from among those with demonstrated success in their own fields of work and proven devotion to the brotherhood and its young people, much good could be accomplished. Such local committees would not be a substitute for parental counsel, but rather a supplement to it.

Mutual Aid is needed to help young people find job openings that meet their particular needs. Mennonite employers of labor need help in finding the kind of employees that fit their specific needs. Brethren within the church may have money to invest and others may be in need of funds, but frequently the two situations are not brought into contact with each other and hence both individuals' problems are unsolved. By means of a central agency such as the Aid Section of the Mennonite Central Committee local committees could be kept informed of both needs and opportunities. A person in one part of the country wanting a job in a Mennonite community in some other part of the country could thus use the central agency to determine whether any opportunities existed.

Local mutual aid committees could be especially helpful in counseling brethren who contemplate moving to another part of the country or to a new community. Such individuals might be directed to small Mennonite communities where congregations are in need of additional families to strengthen the brotherhood.

SUGGESTIONS:

1. Make a list of additional areas in which you think there is need for mutual aid.

2. Make a list of the names, ages, dates of leaving and present addresses of former church members who have left your congregation within the past thirty years. Find the reason for their leaving.

QUESTIONS:

1. Are there promising young people in your congregation who are not making full use of their talents because of lack of funds?

2. How many young people in your congregation have left the community in the past ten years because of a lack of opportunity to start farming in the home community?

3. What plan has your church for seeing that all members of the church have jobs or farming and business opportunities in a Mennonite community?

4. What investment opportunities are there in your community in case men with money should want to invest it?

5. What guidance can the young people of your congregation get within the church in helping them decide what their life work should be?

IX

Organizing Mutual Aid in the Local Community

"I do not mean to be easy upon others and hard upon you, but to equalize the burden, and in the present situation to have your plenty make up for what they need, so that some day their plenty may make up for what you need" . . . II Corinthians 8:13-14. (Goodspeed)

We are chiefly concerned in this pamphlet with mutual aid in the local community because it is in this area and on this level in which we as individuals and groups can do something concrete about problems that face us and about convictions we have about solving such problems. While we should not be oblivious to needs on the state, national and world level, it is, nevertheless, the local communities which are the foundation stones upon which the larger structures are built.

Why Organize?

Many will raise the question as to why mutual aid should be organized. Why should not merely an expression of love and goodwill in a spontaneous way suffice whenever a situation of need arises? Why bother with the machinery of organization? It is true that the spontaneous expression of mutual aid can meet a great many of life's problems but there are a large number of recurring problems which cannot be adequately solved without organization. Organization is essential in our society for any significant undertaking. The early Christians found it necessary to organize to promote the gospel within a few years after the death of Jesus and every worthwhile enterprise today finds it necessary to organize in order to gain its goals. Organization provides for greater efficiency and more systematic handling of a problem.

The reason why it has been found advantageous to organize for the purpose of administering mutual aid in local communities is that the informal type of expression does not operate efficiently and justly in all situations. Spontaneous mutual aid leaves unanswered the question of who is to take the initiative when need arises. Also, it does not determine a uniform kind or amount of assistance that is to be granted those in need. In case of fire or accident, the response from neighbors and friends tends to vary from time to time, depending on the popularity of the person affected as well as on the season of the year. Two men having identical misfortunes, one in the middle of winter and the other in early fall, may receive entirely different kinds of treatment at the hands of their neighbors because during the harvest season, people tend to give generously, while during the winter they give more sparingly.

Spontaneous mutual aid is also insufficient in some communities that are numerically small and economically weak. In such communities, the total resources are often not sufficient to reimburse the individual who has sustained losses due to accident and other misfortunes. An organized plan of mutual aid covering a wide area makes possible the systematic distribution of aid on a just basis for all concerned.

A plan of organizing mutual aid, furthermore, provides a means of supervising assistance given. For instance, if a community decides to raise money and assist a young couple in the purchase of a farm; it is possible by means of organization to determine how much money shall be raised, for what purpose it shall be used, how it shall be repaid and who is to give guidance and counsel to the young couple using the funds.

How Organize?

When recurring needs arise in the community which individual families or congregations cannot satisfactorily meet, it is time to think in terms of organizing a committee to see how such a problem can be taken care of. The procedure normally would be for those individuals who recognize the problem to come together for the purpose of discussion and exchange of ideas on how to meet the problem. All really useful organizations have been formed for the purpose of solving some particular problem. The first thing to do is to analyze the problem in such a way that it can be clearly stated and understood. After the problem is analyzed, it is possible to begin working toward its solution. If the problem in question affects a large number of people and if it is a recurring problem, it is probable that a permanent organization should be formed to deal with it.

For instance, everybody in a community sometime or other

will need medical attention, because all of us are likely to be sick or have an accident in which we need to have medical care. This is an illustration of a recurring problem. It cannot well be solved by one person alone; it is a community problem. Having a doctor or a clinic or hospital is of value to the entire community and for that reason, steps should be taken by local groups to provide medical protection for the community if they do not already have such protection.

Likewise, the matter of recreation is a contemporary problem in our society. People have leisure time and most people need to find some way of spending that time profitably. Idleness is still the devil's workshop. If no wholesome activities exist for people to engage in, there will probably be participation in unwholesome, unprofitable and unchristian activities. Thus, recreation concerns a large percentage of the people in a community, and it is a constantly recurring need. It is not solved once and for always. For this reason, it becomes a matter for the entire community to deal with as a group.

Another illustration of a constantly recurring problem is that of getting young people established in earning a livelihood. All of us must eat and all of us must work to earn a living. If we want to be realistic, we must recognize this problem and be organized locally to meet such needs as people are not able to meet by their own efforts. Youth should, of course, be given every encouragement to solve their own problems, but where that is impossible, it must be remembered that in a multitude of counsellors, there is wisdom, and in unity, there is strength. The resources of the group, whether mental or financial, are always superior to those of the individual.

Perhaps, at first only a committee needs to be appointed to be responsible for the problem. If, however, there are large sums of money involved, and this money needs to be raised and its use supervised for a long period of time, it is best to create a formal organization with the usual officers and committees necessary to meet the particular needs.

On the whole, it is well to remember that all organizations should be simple in the beginning and expand as conditions warrant. It is generally not well to attempt to think of all problems that might arise ahead of time and to draw a blue print of the future, but rather to begin on the basis of immediate needs and develop the organization in light of the growing needs and experiences gained in meeting the more simple problems.

Throughout the country, interested local people want to know how a mutual aid program can be undertaken. A few suggestions will, therefore, be in order. Local church groups, wherever they are, can assume that there will be need for information as to where to get jobs, where to buy livestock and equipment for a farm, where to buy farms, where there are opportunities for business establishments, and where to continue education. Likewise, there will be constant need for financial credit. Sometimes this need will be greater than others, but it can be assumed that there will always be some individuals who need financial assistance.

What Local Church Committees Can Do

First, local committees can make a written list of all jobs that are likely to be available locally. A minimum of detailed information about each job would be valuable, such as the name of the person to be seen about securing the job, and details about wages, hours, living arrangements, and any other questions that the applicant would probably ask when told that a job opening exists. It would be well to be supplied with small cards, size 3 x 5 or 4 x 6, on which each job and the details about it could be listed. Those cards then could be arranged alphabetically and filed in permanent form.

A second major service that local mutual aid committees can render is to list farms that are available for sale or rent in the community where young men should be encouraged to settle. This might apply in the home community or in Mennonite Communities some distance away from the home community. The following suggested form might be used in describing the farms listed:

Location: (Distance from trading center) . . .
 Distance from a Mennonite Church . . .
 Distance from a grade school . . . High School . . .
 Highways: Hard surface . . . Gravel . . . Dirt . . .
Descriptions:
 For Sale . . . Rent . . .
Total no. of acres . . . Cultivated . . . In pasture . . . In woodland . . .
 Approximate sale price . . . Rental price . . .
 Quality of land, fertility, level, drainage, etc.

Crops now being raised:
Approximate cost to equip for operation . . .
Buildings:
  House, state of repair
  No. of rooms . . . Electricity . . . Bath . . . What source of water supply?
  Barns: State of repair
  Dairy equipment . . . How many cows? . . .
  Poultry equipment? . . . Number of hens? . . .
  Other buildings and equipment . . .
Market facilities: (For produce now raised, or produce for which the land is adapted) . . .
Additional remarks:

Two copies of each card might be made; one copy to be kept in the local community and one copy to be sent to a central agency, such as the Aid Section of the Mennonite Central Committee.

A third suggestion is that the local aid committee might study community needs and resources for the establishment of new business opportunities and industries. Investigation might reveal that there was need for such services as those of a barber, a shoemaker, a farm machine repair man, a butcher, a baker, a cannery, work clothing factory, furniture factory, or one of a hundred types of small community industries. A card file on which each of such possible businesses or industries could be described should be kept, each business described on a separate card. On it such information as the following might be recorded:

Location . . .

Distance from a Mennonite Church . . .

Available building to house business or industry, whether for sale or rent:

Approximate rental or sale price of buildings: . . .

Estimated cost of business or the establishment of new industry: . . .

The available labor supply: . . .

The marketing facilities for the product manufactured: . . .

Additional remarks: . . .

Two copies of each of such list should be made, one for the local commitee's use and the other to be sent to the Aid Section of the MCC. In this way, local committees could make their wants known and the Aid Section through its in-

ORGANIZING MUTUAL AID 77

formation files might direct the attention of interested individuals to local committees.

A fourth suggestion for the work of local aid committees is to act as the agency to receive contributions as gifts or loans for the groups central aid organization. In times of need, the local committee might take the initiative in soliciting funds for mutual aid purposes. The local aid committee should be the medium of contact with the Mennonite Central Committee Aid Section or the Conference Aid organization whenever it becomes necessary to work out a local applicant's problem. Sometimes, it is a matter of giving a character reference or of evaluating the soundness of a project for which an applicant desires a loan. Many local committees have already been organized and are at work in many congregations.

If Mennonite communities all over the country establish local Aid Committees or organizations, it will help widely scattered Mennonites to meet each other's needs. Several illustrations will show how local committees may begin to work.

In one Pennsylvania Mennonite community with a church membership of less than sixty, a committee of twelve of the leading men in the church met one afternoon and talked over ways of strengthening their Church membership and their community. In the course of this discussion, they agreed that they needed a medical doctor, a shoemaker, an accountant, a community nurse, an electrician and a mechanic, a garage and repair service station, and three or four married men willing to work on farms. This group of men within the course of a single hour's discussion discovered that by pooling their thinking, they could list job possibilities and business opportunities for eleven people, all of them providing a living for a family. The task of making these needs known, however, still remains to be done. There has been no way of helping this local committee complete its plans.

This small group was so eager to invite a Mennonite doctor to the community that they agreed, if necessary, to raise sufficient money to equip a young physician's office and establish a medical clinic for him. The three or four jobs for farmers were not to be mere jobs as hired men, but were considered as opportunities leading to farm ownership. This community illustrated the need for local committees to study their own needs and community resources and shows what local committees can discover for community betterment when they set their minds to it.

In another Mennonite community, the men from five Mennonite churches which are located relatively close to each other gathered to discuss what they as a larger community group could do to provide employment for their young men after they return from the services and agreed to organize permanently to investigate community resources with special attention to the possibility of establishing new industries.

In a Missouri community where there are three small Mennonite congregations, the bishop in charge held several meetings with representatives from the three churches. Out of these meetings came a decision to survey themselves as to job opportunities, farms for sale or rent, and business openings. The communities were briefly described and the information shared with the Aid Section of M.C.C. This group of churches is eager to attract additional brethren to its congregations.

Certain types of mutual aid can be adequately expressed with perfectly satisfying results without any formal organization. Needs as expressed above can often be met by two individuals. It may require nothing more than to bring together a man with a need and another who has the means to meet this need. This might logically fall under the general heading of counseling. A local aid committee could help others work out many of their problems merely by providing the desired information; that is, to bring together two individuals who have differing but nevertheless, complementary needs. For instance, a promising young man in the local community might be looking for an opportunity to go into farming with the intention of ultimately buying a farm, but at present has very little or no capital with which to begin. His only asset might be good health, good judgment, good character, and a willingness to work diligently in order to meet his obligations. In the same community, there might be an elderly farmer who because of his age was no longer able to do farm work and for that reason is thinking of retiring. Instead of the older man making a public sale and disposing of all his livestock, machinery, and farm for cash and leaving the farm reluctantly after spending most of his lifetime building it up, why shouldn't the retiring farmer and the aspiring young farmer get together and work out a plan whereby the young man can gradually buy out the older one? Such a possibility is not utopian or idealistic. It is practical and realistic. The only thing that needs to be done is to work out a clear cut plan, one that can be understood, agreed to, and easily followed by both parties. Such a plan should be mutually beneficial to the retiring farmer, as well as to the young man wishing to begin. The young man might agree to work as a hired man at a fixed wage plus an opportunity to buy or raise some livestock and crops over a preliminary period of three or four years. During the following five years, the plan might call for a rental arrangement whereby an increasing share in the ownership of livestock and machinery is acquired by the young man. After this initial period, the farm might be taken over by the younger farmer at an agreed upon price mutually arrived at with the help of an impartial appraiser.

Under such a plan the elderly farmer would have the genuine satisfaction of seeing the farm on which he had spent a lifetime building and improving, continue in good hands and getting a young man started under his general supervision. Local mutual aid committees might be the means of consummating such plans. If this were widely practiced throughout the Mennonite communities of the country, acceptable standards and methods would be developed for those individuals wishing to release ownership gradually as well as for those wishing to achieve farm ownership.

Whatever the purpose for which mutual assistance is given and regardless of the formality or informality of the aid, there are certain basic principles that should be kept in mind at all times in carrying out mutual aid practices.

Business Principles

It should be remembered that as disciples of Christ, we want to operate only on the basis of high ethical principles. Mutual aid is a two-way relationship in which all parties concerned should be motivated by the Love of Christ. Mutual aid can be based on sound business principles and still be carried on in a spirit of mutual love. Mutual aid should not be confused with charity or outright relief. It is a program of assistance where the assisted one returns the amount received after he has been given a financial start.

Amount

The amount of financial assistance to any one individual is

not so important as the purpose for which the money is to be used. Amounts of loans should be based on the nature of the project. If a person is deemed worthy of financial assistance, the loan should be large enough to enable the borrower to set up a self-liquidating program. Half-hearted and half-way assistance is often worse than no assistance, because it asks a person to make a success of a venture after placing a handicap on him. Whatever is worth doing is worth doing wisely, but well.

Time

The length of time for repayment of loans is likewise dependent upon the project under consideration. However, the time should be sufficiently long to enable the borrower to make repayments in small amounts at regular intervals. Time is an important factor in helping a man get an economic start.

Interest

The interest rates, if charged at all, should be low. It would be helpful to the borrower if no interest were charged during at least the first year. The cost of a loan to the borrower should be as low as possible, because it is to be remembered that the purpose of mutual aid is to help a brother. The brother making the loan should under no circumstance seek to get a high interest rate at the expense of his brother in need. Where money is borrowed for the purpose of making profit by means of speculation and reinvestment, interest rates are legitimate charges, but where loans are made to a brother to help him get a vocational start, interest charges should be as low as possible or not charged at all.

Security

The basic security of mutual aid loans should be the borrower's word. "Let your communications be yea, yea, and nay, nay." Mutual aid should again seek to establish the tradition of a man's word being as good as his bond. Mutual aid loans then are chiefly character loans which means that the lender has confidence in the integrity and dependability of the borrower to repay. Where funds are used to purchase land, property or equipment, the purchased commodity should serve as additional security.

ORGANIZING MUTUAL AID

Repayment

At the time a mutual aid loan is made the borrower and lender or the mutual aid representative should work out a clearly understood plan of repayment and each retain a written copy. The plan should be based on the expected earnings of the borrower with proper allowance for unforeseen emergencies. Wherever possible, repayments should be amortized, that is, the principle and interest should be calculated in advance and apportioned in fixed payments. This is of help to both parties in the arrangement.

Supervision

Almost as important as the loan itself is wise supervision of its use. Where it is thought advisable the local aid committee might exercise the same thoughtful and careful help that a father would give to his son or a brother to his brother. Wise supervision will not be considered as interference or busybodying, but rather as a friendly inquiry and helpful suggestion.

SUGGESTIONS:

1. Find out all you can about the kind of services performed by local aid committees in other congregations and Mennonite groups.
2. Study and discuss ways in which mutual aid services might be expanded locally or on a Conference wide basis.

QUESTIONS:

1. What are the advantages of an organized mutual aid committee in the local congregation?
2. If you wanted to settle in a new community, how would you decide where to settle?
3. If you wanted to attract other Mennonites to settle in your community, how would you go about it?
4. What useful functions can a mutual aid committee perform in a congregation and in a community?
5. What would you say are fundamental principles in giving financial assistance to a worthy brother in the Church?

X

What Mutual Aid Can Mean to the Church

"If a son shall ask bread of any of you that is a father, will he give him a stone?" Luke 11:11.

In the discussion of mutual aid in the preceding chapters, we have attempted to describe the nature of Christian mutual aid; we have tried to show that it has a Biblical basis and that it has been an integral part of the tradition, custom and heritage of the Mennonite people. We have attempted to indicate in a brief way the types of mutual aid and cooperative activities now being carried on as well as the future needs, and probable opportunities for its development. The basic questions of the "what," "where" and "how" of mutual aid have been discussed. In this concluding chapter, the question— Why mutual aid?—must be answered.

We wish to elaborate here the meaning of mutual aid to the church. This is finally the most important concern of all Christians. Since the church is the institution through which Christ lives and moves and works on earth, we are really asking what mutual aid can mean to the work of Christ. There are at least four significant meanings mutual aid can have for the Christian Church. These are discussed here with particular references to the Mennonite Church because of her conception of the true church as a body of believers based on the apostolic pattern described in the New Testament.

Demonstration of Brotherhood

Mutual aid motivated by the love of Christ in the hearts of professing believers can demonstrate qualities of genuine Christian brotherhood. The world is much more in need of an actual demonstration of brotherhood than it is in need of theorizing longer about it. The world, today as always, is filled with sorrow, pain, suffering, fear and uncertainty. Many are looking for a way out today as they were in the prophet Joel's time. He exclaimed, "Multitudes, multitudes in the valley of decision." They turn to modern churches and many do not find an answer to their plight. The modern church often lacks the spiritual warmth, the spontaneous fervor and radiance that attracts non-believers into its fellowship. There is a need for the spiritual glow in the modern church that characterized the New Testament Christians to such an extent that pagans enviously remarked, "Behold, how they love one another." Paul said to the Corinthians, "I will show you a far better way." He was referring to the way of the Christ instead of the way of the world. It is our duty to point to that "better way."

The development of a mutual aid consciousness in the brotherhood will result in its strengthening. If motivated by the love of Christ, Christian groups can be effective witnesses to the way of Christ. Mutual aid is a demonstration, not a theory; it is a way of preaching love and goodwill with deeds instead of words. The world needs just that. Thousands of local congregations need to leaven thousands of local communities. If brotherhood is to grow internationally, it must grow locally.

Develop Loyalty of Youth For the Church

The development of mutual aid within our local congregations and within our groups as a whole will mean that we can count on a greater degree of loyalty and solidarity. Young people respect and support the church to about the same degree that the church helps them. If the church helps its young people, the young people will support the church.

This evidence of loyalty has been demonstrated in Mennonite circles in Russia and in Mexico. Here the church assumed responsibility for finding land and job opportunites so that its young people did not need to forsake their community for the sake of a job. A program of mutual aid provides for a way of getting young people started locally, so that they can remain members of their home church, or if local opportunities do not exist, it helps them locate in other Mennonite communities where opportunities do exist. If necessary, Mennonite groups can establish new colonies by means of mutual aid, whereby the church is planted in the new settlement and new religious growth started. In this way, mutual aid helps provide a basis on which youth can be loyal to the church and it shows how mutual aid promotes the total purpose of the church.

If the church uses brotherhood only as an ideal without giving reality to its meaning, youth will forsake the church and worship at other altars. The altar at which it will most likely worship, if not at the church altar, will be the altar of the State.

The government is rendering to its citizens increasingly more services, in addition to the traditional services of protection by law, insurance against injustice and maintenance of public utilities. Today, the government provides hospital service, education from kindergarten to university and, at the present time, a social security program to protect citizens from economic want from the cradle to the grave. Social security means the guarantee of jobs and at least a minimum cash income on which a person may live. There are employment offices in every state and many counties of the Union, and every state has some form of old age pension. In this situation and with trends moving in this direction, it is very easy for our young people to turn away from the church to the state for all their needs. In so doing, they will view the church as of increasingly less significance. Hence, unless the situation is changed, one may expect to find Mennonites in time to become as indifferent to religion and as inactive in church work as is characteristic of a large segment of secularized America today.

No one who is seriously interested in promoting the welfare of the church and the cause which it represents, wishes to see this trend away from the church. It is, therefore, not only desirable, but very urgent that the church establish a mutual aid program locally and denomination-wide for the purpose of assisting all brethren, old and young, who are in need of such assistance. The practice of the early Christians as described in the Third Epistle of John, seventh verse, is still practical and applicable in the case of the Mennonites. "For His Name's sake they went forth, taking nothing of the Gentiles."

Reduce Materialistic Practices Among Church Members

One of the serious defects of modern Christianity is its adoption of a philosophy of materialistic individualism. Mennonites by and large are as guilty of this as most other Christian groups. The only difference is that they adopted it more recently. This means in a more simple language, that individual Christians have accepted the worldly view that it is every man's right to accumulate as much wealth as he can and spend it in any way he pleases without regard to what others may think, do or need. Materialism is a view which measures everything in dollars and cents. It has little or no regard for the value of the unseen or spiritual things. This is basically a pagan, not a Christian philosophy.

The tragedy of the situation today is that we find many Christians who roundly condemn materialism and, at the same time, embrace it. We are all guilty of this to a larger degree than we can properly justify before Christ and our commitments to him. This is especially significant for Mennonites in the light of our profession that true Christianity is characterized by its simplicity, its non-conformity and its renunciation of pride in favor of humility and holy obedience. Many of our practices when examined in the light of these professions are likely to leave us somewhat embarrassed.

This materialistic philosophy has developed slowly and subtly. It has been adopted along with many other secular and worldly practices on the basis of a little here and a little there until the whole of life has been beclouded with it. Materialistic practices have become so habitual that many brethren vigorously defend them as though they were an inherent part of the Christian philosophy.

It is unfortunate that in general, our Mennonite business men and manufacturers who employ hired help have not distinguished themselves for their Christian way of dealing with employees. So far as our observations are concerned, we have been able to see little difference between the attitude and treatment of employees by Mennonite employers than those of any other Christian or non-Christian employers. The element of mutuality has been much more at the periphery than at the center of employer-employee relations.

The New Testament principle described in the Book of Acts as the brethren helping each according to his ability and each according to his need has not been the principle on which business has operated. Christians have accepted very much, the standards of the commercial world. The charging of interest, the level of wages, the foreclosure of mortgages, the opposition to improvement of the conditions of the working man, our indifference to racial discrimination and the development of class consciousness because of large differences in wealth within our own brotherhood have developed gradually and without opposition from the church. These evidences of secularism and materialism within the Mennonite brotherhood account for the loss of the practice of mutual aid.

A program of mutual aid whereby we are made continually conscious of our obligations one to another and where we are engaged in actively helping each other in the Name of Christ will eliminate much of selfish materialism. Christian love applied to economic relations will change these practices. It would be a fitting testimony if pagans of our day would be able to say of our brethren who employ labor and who engage in business, as well as those who serve as individual job holders, "Behold, how they make the crooked places straight and the rough places plain."

Makes Dependence Upon the State less Necessary

The development of a mutual aid program among Mennonites can be one of the most effective demonstrations that we still believe in the traditional principle of separation of church and state. Our fathers bought this principle at the cost of much blood and suffering. We are today in danger of surrendering the principle because of much prosperity and comfort. The relationship between church and state today is so congenial that we find it difficult to resist when the state encroaches on the domain of the church, and in fact we have been encouraging the state to take over the responsibilities that were formerly discharged by the church as was indicated in the preceding section. The present danger of further regimentation of life by a proposed program of compulsory universal military training for war is one of the foreshadows that should make us apprehensive. The increasing demand of the state over the life of individual citizens will gradually lead to a totalitarian state and in a totalitarian state, the church is no longer free and independent. It becomes a servant of the state.

The establishment of a practical program of mutual aid within the church is one of the most effective ways of counteracting the threat of statism in America. Statism is a religion not unlike emperor worship of early Roman days. The state sets itself up as the ultimate authority, demands absolute obedience, and in time of war requires the equivalent of worship in its zeal for evidences of patriotism.

A program of mutual aid gives strength to the church and provides a way of escape from ever increasing economic and social dependence upon the government. It is one way of stemming the current trend toward state regimentation. Perhaps most significant of all, it releases individuals from a sense of moral obligation to the state in return for the material security and gratuities offered by the government. People who are dependent upon the state for bread and butter, health, education, and economic security from the cradle to the grave will in the long run also tend to look to it for guidance and direction in other matters. As the state increases in importance, the church will decrease. Economic security apart from the church may mean spiritual indifference to the church. A program of mutual aid motivated by the Love of Christ will encourage men to look for guidance and direction to Christ and His followers rather than to Caesar. It is a way of testifying that Mennonites still believe in the separation of church and state.

Conclusion

The purpose of all Christian mutual aid from the Mennonite standpoint is that it should strengthen the cause of Christ in the local community. Unless it serves this purpose, it misses the mark entirely. Christian mutual aid has both its beginning and its end in the body of Christ. It is the way through which the Love of Christ manifests itself in the lives of His disciples. For then it is the natural expression of their love for Him and for each other. It is not artificial or compulsory, but rather the spontaneous outpouring of the true Christian's desire to share and serve. It is the natural expression of love in action of the spiritually reborn Christian.

When enough individuals allow this love to affect their everyday relations, the neighborhood and the community will gradually feel its effects. For this reason, the church is primarily interested in helping its young people become vocationally established in communities where there are Mennonite churches. In this way, it is able to build socially solid and spiritually strong Christian groups which in turn become industrious and law-abiding communities.

A fully developed program of mutual aid is really only the fulfillment of the ideals of the church in the week-day lives of its members. It is carrying out the injunction of doing unto others as you would that they should do unto you. Both to the believer and non-believer, it is an attempt to heed Isaiah's admonition to, "Prepare ye the way of the Lord, make straight in the desert a highway for our God."

SUGGESTIONS:

1. Make a list of illustrations showing how the state is today performing functions formerly performed by the Church.

2. Define materialism and make a list of practices in our world which you would call materialistic.

QUESTIONS:

1. What changes might take place in the Mennonite Church if a genuine program of Christian mutual aid were developed?

2. Is it possible to practice brotherhood in business and yet face competition successfully?

3. What evidences are there that the Church and State are not as "separate" as they once were?

4. Do you believe a well developed program of mutual aid would win greater loyalty from the young people to the Mennonite Church?

5. How could Christian mutual aid combat the materialistic trend of our times?

Reading References

BOOKS

Coady, M. M. *Masters of Their Own Destiny.* New York: Harper, 1939.
: A well written and easily read little book on cooperatives. It discusses the development of a cooperative program among poor Nova Scotia fishermen as promoted by the Catholic Church.

Dawson, C. A. *Group Settlement: Ethnic Communities in Western Canada.* Toronto: Macmillan Co., 1936.
: Contains a splendid section on the Mennonites in Manitoba.

Gingerich, M., *Mennonites in Iowa.* Torch Press for the State Historical Society of Iowa, Iowa City, Iowa.

Contains excellent chapters on church and community life which include both the spirit and practice of Christian cooperation.

Hershberger, G. F., *War, Peace and Nonresistance*. The Herald Press, Scottdale, Pennsylvania, 1944.
The final chapter of this widely read book discusses the place and importance of mutual aid in the Christian community.

Infield, Henrich, F., *Cooperative Communiites at Work*. The Dryden Press, New York, 1945.
A study of how cooperative communites of various types have operated in times past and how they are functioning at the present time.

Mead, Margaret, *Cooperation and Competition Among Primitive Peoples*. New York: McGraw-Hill, 1937.
A scholarly study of the factors and forces of competition and cooperation in several primitive Island Societies.

Schmiedler, Edgar, *Cooperation—A Christian Mode of Industry*. New Publishers—St. Nazianz, Wisconsin, 1941.
The story of cooperative principles and practices is sympathetically told. Special emphasis is laid on the ethical nature of cooperative practices.

ARTICLES

Kreider, Carl, "The Economic Program of the Mennonite Community of Tommorrow," *Mennonite Quarterly Review*. XIX (April, 1945) 143-155.
A useful supplementary article for understanding the background of mutual aid problems.

Mumaw, John R. "Current Forces Adversely Affecting the Life of the Mennonite Community," *Mennonite Quarterly Review*, (April, 1945) 101-116.
The title of the article is descriptive of the contents.

Bender, Harold S., "The Mennonite Conception of the Church and Its Relation to Present Day needs," *Mennonite Quarterly Review*, (April 1945) 90-100.
A good brief statement of the Nature of the Mennonite Concept of the Church.

Fretz, J. Winfield, "Mutual Aid Among the Mennonites, I," *Mennonite Quarterly Review*. XIII (January, 1939), 28-58.
A discussion of the religious principles underlying Mennonite mutual aid with material out of Mennonite history to illustrate the principle and practice.

———. "Mutual Aid among the Mennonites, II," *Mennonite Quarterly Review*, XIII (July, 1939) 187-209.
A study of the mutual aid activities in Mountain Lake Minnesota.

———. "Mennonites and Their Economic Problems," *Mennonite Quarterly Review*, XIV (October, 1940), 195-213.
An analysis of economic problems facing Mennonites with suggestions for solution along mutual aid lines.

———. "Recent Community Building in Canada," *Mennonite*

Quarterly Review, XVIII (January, 1944) 5-21.
An account of observations of mutual aid activities in Mennonite communities in Canada from Ontario to British Columbia.

———. *Mennonite Colonization,* Mennonite Central Committee, Akron, Pennsylvania. 1944.
A pamphlet discussing the causes of success and failure of Mennonite colonization in the past with suggestions for the future.

———. *Mennonite Colonization in Mexico.* Mennonite Central Committee, Akron, Pennsylvania, 1945.
A brief pamphlet describing life and activity of Old Colony Mennonites in Mexico—contains useful lessons for American Mennonites.

Hershberger, Guy F. "Suggestions for Improving the Small Christian Community," *Proceedings of the First Conference on Mennonite Cultural Problems.* 1942.
Published by the Council of Mennonite and Affiliated Colleges.

———. "Maintaining the Mennonite Rural Community," *Mennonite Quarterly Review.* XIV (October, 1940), 214-223.
Discusses mutual aid as one of the requirements for a strong rural community.

www.ingramcontent.com/pod-product-compliance
Lightning Source LLC
Chambersburg PA
CBHW070324100426
42743CB00011B/2545